WOMEN
VS
MEN

Why Women Are
Better Than Men

Women start here

LESLEY RIDDOCH

BLACK & WHITE PUBLISHING

First published 2004
by Black & White Publishing Ltd
99 Giles Street, Edinburgh EH6 6BZ

ISBN 1 84502 021 9

British Library Cataloguing in Publication Data:
A catalogue record for this book is available
from the British Library.

Cover illustration by Bob Dewar

Printed and bound in Denmark by AIT Nørhaven A/S

CONTENTS

ACKNOWLEDGEMENTS

Thanks to the guys and gals who contributed –
Susie Lang, Jean Rafferty, Graham Burgess, Lesley Quirk,
Miranda Hurst, Fiona MacDonald, Alcia Thomas, Lorraine
Illingworth, Prof Sara Carter, The Diary at the Herald, Joan
McFadden, Jackie Brierton, Dorothy Grace Elder, Katie
Ferguson, Zin Craig and Chris Smith – in my book,
the only husband worth having.

WOMEN vs MEN

INTRODUCTION

STOP PRESS
The First Minister of Scotland wants to encourage skilled Europeans to come and live north of the border. But Jack McConnell's valiant effort is getting nowhere fast. So the multilingual Big Man has introduced Euro-grammar to the Scottish language to make foreigners feel more at hame. Henceforth, nouns will have a gender as they do in France, Germany, Italy, Spain, etc., etc. Thus *la noblesse* – nobility – is obviously feminine while *le merde* – crap – is clearly masculine. So Jack set up a committee and a review and after three consultations has decided the following:

Monday
Male because it always comes too soon.

Encyclopedia Britannica
Male because it knows everything and is never wrong.

Passenger
Female because it's generally picked up by the same old lines.

Kidneys
Female because they always go to the toilet in pairs.

Tyres
Male because they go bald and are over inflated.

Sponges
Female because they are soft, squeezable and retain water.

Photocopier
Female because, once turned off, they take a long time to warm up.

Shoes
Male because they are generally unpolished with their tongues hanging out.

Scottish Parliament Building
Female because it cost more and took longer to get ready than anyone expected apart from . . .

God
Female. Because.

1

NO GREAT SHAKES – THAT DON'T IMPRESS ME MUCH . . .

Let's face it, if men were designed to be human peacocks displaying fantastically coloured, well-toned hind-quarters before awed clutches of dowdy peahens, the creative team failed. It doesn't take a bad case of builder's bum to persuade most women that men aren't even trying when they strut their stuff. But try telling the men that.

I once watched a stage hypnotist persuade four Glaswegian men and women they were stark naked. The two women raced for the stage curtains and dived in. The two Rab C lookalikes paraded round the stage – admiring audience on one side, massive hypnotic penises on the other. In their heads.

Despite all evidence to the contrary, men think they are God's gift to women. Why was country singer Shania Twain's career transformed with her hit single 'That Don't Impress Me Much'? Because she was speaking for a hundred per cent of female humanity. In THAT desert video, Shania not only played the perfect peacock (now THOSE are outfits boys), she also looked male posturing straight in the eye (even Brad Pitt's) and remained thoroughly underwhelmed.

This is the modern wummin, guys – well, OK, Shania is a bit special on the outside – but inside we ordinary gals also ain't impressed with displays of muscle we can now acquire in gyms, cars we've already bought and good looks that invariably come with major ego problems. God, I'm scaring myself.

The only thing we really need from you guys is . . . well that would be telling.

Collected from the ceiling of the Gynaecology clinic in Edinburgh Royal Infirmary. Don't ask!

15 reasons why dogs are better than men

Dogs don't have problems expressing affection in public.

Dogs miss you when you have gone.

Dogs feel guilt when they've done something wrong.

Dogs don't brag about who they've just slept with.

Dogs don't criticise your friends.

Dogs admit when they're jealous.

Dogs don't feel threatened by your intelligence.

Dogs understand what 'no' means.

You can housetrain a dog.

Middle-aged dogs don't feel the need to trade you for a younger owner.

Dogs don't mind if you do all the driving.

Dogs don't step on an imaginary brake if you do any driving – or look pointedly at their watches just before you deliver the punchline to a joke.

Dogs admit when they are lost.

Dogs don't feel threatened if you earn more than they do.

Dogs mean it when they kiss you.

A fairy tale for the woman of the twenty-first century
Once upon a time in a land far away, a beautiful, independent, self-assured princess happened upon a frog as she sat contemplating ecological issues on the shores of an unpolluted loch in a verdant meadow near her castle.

The frog hopped into the princess's lap and said, 'Elegant lady, I was once a handsome prince until an evil witch cast a spell upon me. One kiss from you, however, and I will turn back into the dapper young prince that I am and then, my sweet, we can marry and set up house in your castle with my mother, where you can prepare my meals, clean my clothes, bear my children and forever feel happy and grateful doing so.'

That night, as the princess dined sumptuously on a repast of lightly sautéed frogs legs in a white wine sauce, she chuckled to herself and said, 'I don't frigging think so!'

Why are men like popcorn?
They satisfy you but only for a little while.

Why are men are like tablemats?
They only show up when there's food on the table.

Why are men like mascara?
They usually run at the first sign of emotion.

Why are men like bike helmets?
They're handy in an emergency but, otherwise, they just look silly.

Why are men like government bonds?
They take so long to mature.

Why are men like parking places?
The good ones are taken and the rest are too small.

Why are men like photocopiers?
You need them for reproduction but that's about it.

Why are men like lava lamps?
They're fun to look at but not all that bright.

Why are men like high heels?
They're easy to walk on once you get the hang of it.

Why are men like bananas?
The older they get, the less firm they become.

What's the difference between men and pigs?
Pigs don't turn into men when they drink.

2
GROSS BEHAVIOUR

Gross is one of those old-fashioned, spinstery words that nonetheless captures the biggest problem with men (next to basic stupidity, sex obsession, etc.) Guys, you do such yuck things. In public. Without shame. Over and over. Why is it no surprise to find most food poisoning comes from peanuts in bars dished out by men who've specially peed on their hands before serving them? Why not? The idea that noble kings of the jungle could be reduced to mere service simply flies in the face of nature.

Just as dogs in heat must try to mount your leg and male cats must pee to the right of the fireplace, men must be gross. It's marking territory to them, girls. Lighting farts, gobbing competitions, peeing on toilet seats, ball shuffling (for which coin rattling eventually becomes the middle-aged substitute) – they have to do it. And then complain bitterly about women breastfeeding in public. Still, it must help police to know they can safely eliminate 51% of humanity from inquiries into crimes of public decency.

They have to test the limits, girls – and we have to hand them the Domestos and the black bin bags.

Q. Why do men whistle when they're sitting on the toilet?
A. Because it helps them remember which end they need to wipe.

He says, 'Let's try a new position tonight.'
She says, 'OK, you stand at the ironing board for three hours and I'll sit on the sofa and fart.

Why men are gross – or why it is good to be a woman
Taxis stop for us because we rarely hold them up or throw up over the driver.

We don't have to pass wind to amuse ourselves.

If we forget to shave, no one knows.

We can congratulate a teammate without ever touching her bottom.

We never have to make sure our privates are still there in public.

We don't look like frogs in blenders when dancing.

We can talk to the opposite sex without having to picture them naked.

We will never regret piercing our ears.

There are times when chocolate really can solve all our problems.

We can say all this in the presence of men because they aren't listening anyway.

Q. Why do female black widow spiders kill their males after mating?
A. To stop the snoring before it starts.

Last week we took some of our friends out to a new restaurant run by seven men. They had all graduated from business school together and believed that, without the distraction of women, they could apply logic to the art of cookery.

I noticed the waiter carried a spoon in his shirt pocket. When the wine waiter brought our water and cutlery, he had a spoon in his top pocket. Then I looked around and saw all seven men had spoons in their top pockets. When the waiter returned, I asked why.

'Well,' he explained, 'after several months of analysis, we concluded that the spoon was the most frequently dropped utensil. If we carry a spare, we can reduce the number of trips back to the kitchen and save fifteen man-hours per shift.'

I was impressed. I also noticed a string hanging out of the waiter's fly. Looking around, I saw all seven waiters had the same string hanging from their flies. So, before he walked off, I asked why.

'We also found we can save time in the toilets. By fixing this string to the tip of you-know-what, we can pull it out without touching it and eliminate the need to wash our hands, shortening loo time by 76.39 percent.'

I asked, 'After you get it out, how do you put it back?'

'Well,' he whispered, 'I don't know about the others but I use the spoon.'

A man is in a crowded lift and shouts, 'Ballroom, please.'

A woman in front of him turns around and says, 'I'm sorry, I didn't realise I was crowding you.'

3
LAZY

Now we're talking. So, guys, just shut it. There is no argument with the facts. Across the world women do 70% of the work and own 10% of the wealth. OK, so maybe the wealth pendulum's slowly swinging the other way in the West. Live with it – or sponsor a mum in Kampala.

Why do women put up with it? Well, recent research suggests that, again, male laziness may be involuntary and linked to the modern growth of multitasking.

Guys, that's putting the kettle on for tea AND getting biscuits. You can do that sometimes. OK. How about an average female multitask – simultaneously driving the car, text messaging the work, lowering the car window and collecting enough snow from the roof to dampen a make-up sponge prior to careful application? C'mon, guys, give up. Seriously – real, proper male scientists have found that women have multitasking sewn up. We have specific areas of the brain to control speech. So, when a woman is talking, the rest of her brain is available for other tasks. A man, it seems, doesn't have one specific speech HQ. So his whole brain seizes up with the effort of uttering one sentence. A woman has better links between the hemispheres of her brain. That means we are better at spotting lies – mismatches between verbal and non-verbal signals using both sides of the old grey matter.

So, guys, if you must tell porkies, try it over the phone where we can't see you making a hash of it!

Q. How many honest, intelligent, caring men in the world does it take to do the dishes?
A. Both of them.

Q. How does a man show that he is planning for the future?
A. He buys two cases of beer.

Q. How many men does it take to change a roll of toilet paper?
A. We don't know – it has never happened.

The Male Rules of the workplace
We've been led to believe men are the pulsing, aggressive go-getters of the business world. In most workplaces the truth is very different . . .

Men waste time, so women don't have to.

A woman does the job RIGHT the first time and gets the job done. A man does the job WRONG fourteen times and gets a job for life.

Lazy Men Mottoes

Eagles may soar but sloths don't get sucked into jet engines.

Artificial Intelligence is no match for Natural Stupidity.

Plagiarism saves time.

Never put off until tomorrow what you can avoid altogether.

TEAMWORK means never taking the blame.

Retirement is only thirty years away.

Aim low, reach your goals, avoid disappointment.

According to the Alaska Department of Fish and Game, female reindeer keep their antlers till they give birth in the spring while male reindeer drop their antlers at the beginning of winter. So, according to every historical account of Santa's reindeer, every single one of them, from Rudolph to Blitzen, had to be a girl.

We should've known. Only pregnant women would be expected to drag a fat man in a red velvet suit all around the world in one night, and not get lost.

4
STUPID

The jury is out on this one. Are men stupid or very, very clever indeed? By pretending to be thick how many duff jobs do they escape? By needing to prove we can cope with everything, how many duff jobs do women take on? And who's the winner at the end of the day – the knackered but triumphant woman or the guy who got what he really wanted . . . not a diploma in re-heating a can of macaroni but half an hour of quiet to watch the footie with his feet up? My mum may not recall making a formative observation when I was wee. 'Never learn to type,' said she, 'you'll end up a typist for some stupid guy.' The two fingered typing that has produced this side of the book shows that I listened to her – on that subject at least.

So are men stupid or cleverly failing to learn things that would give them more work? I favour the conspiracy theory on this one. Take workmen. Yes, girls, we must. Either they fail to use diaries because they think wee books look poofy and prefer to live with hacked off customers on their backs all day – that's the stupid option. Or they have figured out that ducking and weaving keeps us on the back foot, puts them in charge and eventually swells their wallets because we will eventually pay ANYTHING just to get one in the house for more than ten minutes – that's the evil but clever option.

Ladies, as the foreman said, take your pick.

When God created Adam, He told him the good news – he'd been given a brain and a penis. The bad news? He only had a big enough blood supply to use one at a time.

Why do men like a BMW? They can spell it.

Q. *What's the difference between a computer and a man?* A. You only have to punch instructions into a computer once!

A husband read an article to his wife about how many words women use a day – 30,000 to a man's 15,000. The wife replied, 'That's because we have to repeat everything to men.'

He said, 'What?'

A man said to his wife, 'I don't know how you can be so stupid and so beautiful all at the same time.' The wife responded, 'Allow me to explain. God made me beautiful so you would be attracted to me; God made me stupid so I would be attracted to you!'

A man walks into a chemist and wanders around. The sales girl notices him and asks if she can help. He answers that he needs a box of tampons for his wife.

She directs him to the right shelf. A few minutes later, he dumps a huge bag of cotton balls and a ball of string on the counter.

She says, confused, 'Sir, I thought you were looking for some tampons for your wife?'

He answers, 'Yesterday, I sent my wife to the store to get me a carton of cigarettes and she came back with a tin of tobacco and some rolling papers; 'cause it's sooooooooooo much cheaper. You know, she's right. So, I figure if I have to roll my own . . . '

A couple drove down a country road for several miles, not saying a word. An earlier discussion had led to an argument and neither of them wanted to concede their position.

As they passed a farmyard of mules, goats, and

pigs, the husband asked sarcastically, 'Relatives of yours?'

'Yep,' the wife replied, 'in-laws.'

Stupid Men Quotes
'I've never had major knee surgery on any other part of my body.'
Winston Bennett, University of Kentucky basketball forward

'Half this game is ninety percent mental.'
Danny Ozark, Philadelphia Phillies manager

'The word "genius" isn't applicable in football. A genius is a guy like Norman Einstein.'
Joe Theisman, NFL football quarterback

'We don't necessarily discriminate. We simply exclude certain types of people.'
Colonel Gerald Wellman, ROTC Instructor

'If we don't succeed, we run the risk of failure.'
Bill Clinton

'We are ready for an unforeseen event that may or may not occur.'
Al Gore, Vice President

After a woman gave birth, the doctor stood solemnly beside the bed. 'There is something I must tell you about your baby.'

'What's wrong?' the alarmed mother asked.

'Your baby is a hermaphrodite.'

'What's that?'

'It means your baby has both male and female parts.'

'Oh my God, that's wonderful!' the mother said. 'You mean it has a penis and a brain?'

A blind man enters a lesbian bar by mistake. He finds his way to a bar stool and orders a drink. After sitting there for a while, he yells to the bartender, 'Hey, you wanna hear a blonde joke?' The bar immediately falls absolutely quiet.

In a very deep, husky voice, the woman next to him says, 'Before you tell that joke, sir, you should know five things:

1. The bartender is a blonde girl
2. The bouncer is a blonde girl
3. I'm a 6-feet-tall, 200-pound blonde woman with a black belt in karate
4. The woman sitting next to me is blonde and is a professional weightlifter
5. The lady to your right is a blonde and is a professional wrestler.

Now, think about it seriously, mister. Do you still wanna tell that joke?'

The blind man thinks for a second, shakes his head and declares, 'Nah, not if I'm gonna have to explain it five times.'

Q. Why are most blonde jokes so short?
A. So men can remember them.

Q. What do you call the useless flap of skin on the end of a penis?
A. A man.

Q. Why is it difficult to find men who are sensitive, caring and good looking?
A. They already have boyfriends.

Q. Why does it take one million sperm to fertilise one egg?
A. They won't stop and ask directions.

5
SEX-OBSESSED

Gals, it takes a long time to realise the stories are true – men never stop thinking about sex, surfing to view simulated sex and nudging partners bottoms whilst asleep for unconscious sex (what is it about 5.30am, guys?) Porn is the world's biggest business – and *thinking* about sex clearly gets men on a high. Shame the same can't be said for their sperm count.

But actually *having* sex is a very different thing. More often that not drink, has been taken big-time and it's a case of all hands on deck to raise the mast (so to speak). Thereafter the gentle curves of the billowing sails are all too easily overlooked by the snoring male who, if prodded sharply, will apply techniques evidently modelled on deck-scrubbing, barrel-rolling and mainsail hoisting. Even this modest contribution to female satisfaction lapses with time.

No wonder women are blessed with extreme manual dexterity. Ahem.

MAN SPEAK

Do you want to go to a film? = I'd eventually like to have sex with you.

May I have this dance? = I'd eventually like to have sex with you.

Can I call you sometime? = I'd eventually like to have sex with you.

I love you = Let's have sex now.

This singles ad appeared in *The Atlanta Journal*:
SINGLE BLACK FEMALE seeks male companion-ship, ethnicity unimportant. I'm a very good-looking girl who LOVES to play. I love long walks in the woods, riding in your pickup truck, hunting, camping and fishing trips, cosy winter nights lying by the fire. Candlelight dinners will have me eating out of your hand. Rub me the right way and watch me respond. I'll be at the front door when you get home from work, wearing only what nature gave me. Kiss me and I'm yours. Call (404) 875-6420 and ask for Daisy.

Over 15,000 men found themselves talking to the Atlanta Humane Society about an eight-week-old black Labrador retriever.

Men are so easy.

A woman was sitting at a bar enjoying an after work cocktail with her girlfriends when an exceptionally tall, handsome, sexy man entered. He was so striking that the woman could not take her eyes off him. The man noticed her overly attentive stare and walked directly toward her. (As men will.) Before she could offer her apologies for staring, he leaned over and whispered, 'I'll do anything, absolutely anything, that you want me to do, no matter how kinky, for £100 – on one condition.' (There are always conditions.)

Flabbergasted, the woman asked what the condition was. The man replied, 'You have to tell me what you want me to do in just three words.' (Controlling, eh?)

The woman considered his proposition for a moment, then slowly removed five £20 notes from her purse, which she pressed into the man's hand along with her address. She looked deeply into his eyes and slowly and meaningfully said, 'Clean my house.'

A man goes to the doctor because he is having trouble getting an erection. The doctor says his pelvic muscles have been damaged and the only option is experimental treatment – implanting elephant trunk tissue in the man's penis.

He thinks it over and can't face life without a sex life. So, reassured there will be no cruelty to the elephant, the operation goes ahead.

A few weeks later he's out with his girlfriend at a posh restaurant to celebrate. But, halfway through the meal, a pain between his legs is so fierce he has to unzip his trousers and immediately his penis springs out, grabs a bread roll and returns to his pants.

His girlfriend is speechless. But then with a sly smile she asks, 'Can you do that again?'

With watering eyes the man says, 'I think so but I'm not sure I can fit another roll up my arse.'

A housewife takes a lover during the day, while her husband is at work. Unbeknown to her, her nine-year-old son is hiding in the walk-in wardrobe. Her husband comes home unexpectedly so she hides her lover in the wardrobe. The boy now has company.

Boy: 'Dark in here.'
Man: 'Yes, it is.'
Boy: 'I have a football.'
Man: 'That's nice.'
Boy: 'Want to buy it?'
Man: 'No thanks.'
Boy: 'My dad's outside.'
Man: 'OK, how much?'

Boy: '£50.'

A few weeks later, it all happens again.

Boy: 'Dark in here.'

Man: 'Yes, it is.'

Boy: 'I have some football boots.'

Man: 'How much?'

Boy: '£200.'

Man: 'Fine.'

A few days later, the father says to the boy, 'Grab the ball and your boots. Let's go outside and play keepie uppie.'

The boy says, 'I can't. I sold them.'

The father asks, 'How much did you sell them for?'

The son says, '£250.'

The father says, 'That's terrible to take advantage of your friends like that. I'm taking you to see Father Joseph at the church – he'll make you confess.'

They go to the church and the boy sits in the confession booth and closes the door.

The boy says, 'Dark in here.'

The priest says, 'Don't start that shit again.'

Q. What is the difference between men and women?
A. A woman wants one man to satisfy her every need.
A man wants every woman to satisfy his one need.

A man takes the day off work and decides to go out golfing. He is on the second hole when he notices a frog sitting next to the green. He thinks nothing of it and is about to play when he hears, 'Ribbit, nine iron.' The man looks around and doesn't see anyone. Again, he hears, 'Ribbit, nine iron.'

He looks at the frog and decides to prove the frog wrong, puts the club away and grabs a nine iron. Boom! He hits it ten inches from the cup. He is shocked. He says to the frog, 'Wow that's amazing. You must be a lucky frog, eh?'

The frog replies, 'Ribbit, lucky frog.'

The man decides to take the frog with him to the next hole. 'What do you think, frog?' the man asks.

'Ribbit, three wood.'

The guy takes out a three wood and boom! Hole in one. The man is amazed and doesn't know what to say. By the end of the day, the man has played the best game of his life and asks the frog, 'OK, where to next?'

The frog replies, 'Ribbit, Las Vegas.'

They go to Las Vegas and the guy says, 'OK, frog, now what?'

The frog says, 'Ribbit, roulette.'

Upon approaching the roulette table, the man asks, 'What do you think I should bet?'

The frog replies, 'Ribbit, $3000, black six.'

Now, this is a million-to-one shot to win but, after the golf game, the man figures, 'What the heck?'

Boom! Tons of cash comes sliding back across the table. The man takes his winnings and pays for the best room in the hotel. He sits the frog down and says, 'Frog, I don't know how to repay you. You've won me all this money and I am forever grateful.'

The frog replies, 'Ribbit, kiss me.'

He figures, 'Why not? – after all the frog has done for me, he deserves it.'

With the kiss, the frog turns into a gorgeous fifteen-year-old girl.

'And that, your honour, is how the girl ended up in my room. So help me God.'

(Aye right!)

An Irish lad at confession says, 'Bless me, Father, for I have sinned. I have been with a loose woman.'

The priest asks, 'Is that you, little Danny McGuinness?'

'Yes, Father, it's me.'

'And who was the woman you were with?'

'I can't tell you, Father. I don't want to ruin her reputation.'

'Well, Danny, I'm sure to find out sooner or later so you may as well tell me now. Was it Brenda McLaughlin?'

'I cannot say.'

'Was it Patricia Kelly?'

'I'll never tell.'

'Was it Marie Shannon?'

'I'm sorry but I'll not name her.'

'Was it Mary Catherine Morgan?'

'My lips are sealed, Father.'

'Was it Fiona McDonald, then?'

'Please, Father, I cannot tell you.'

The priest sighs in frustration. 'You're a steadfast lad, Danny McGuinness, and I admire that. But you've sinned and you must atone. You cannot attend church for three months. Off ye go now.'

Danny walks back to his pew. His friend Patrick slides over and whispers, 'What'd you get?'

Danny replies, 'Three months' holiday and five good leads.'

After a long night of making love, the young guy rolled over, pulled out a cigarette from his jeans and searched for his lighter. Unable to find it, he asked the girl if she had one at hand.

'There might be some matches in the top drawer,' she replied.

He opened the drawer of the bedside table and found a box of matches sitting neatly on top of a framed picture of another man. Naturally, the guy began to worry. 'Is this your husband?' he inquired nervously.

'No, silly,' she replied, snuggling up to him.

'Your boyfriend then?' he asked.

'No, not at all,' she said, nibbling away at his ear.

'Well, who is he then?' demanded the bewildered guy.

Calmly, the girl replied, 'That's me before the operation.'

One night a guy takes his girlfriend home. As they are about to kiss each other goodnight at the front door, the guy starts feeling a little horny. With an air of confidence, he leans with his hand against the wall and smiling into her eyes says, 'Darling, let's have sex right here, right now.'

Horrified, she replies, 'Are you mad? My parents will see us!'

'Oh, come on! Who's going to see us?' he asks, grinning persuasively.

'No, please. Can you imagine if we get caught?'

'Oh, come on! There's nobody around – they're all sleeping!'

'No way. It's just too risky!'

'Oh, please, please, I love you so much!'

'No, no and no. I love you too but I just can't!'

'Oh, yes you can.'

'No I can't.'

Suddenly the light on the stairs goes on and her Dad appears in his pyjamas, hair ruffled and, in a sleepy voice, he says, 'Go ahead - have sex but for God's sake, get your hand aff the door entry button!'

6
CRAP CHAT-UP LINES

Scotsmen have an unfortunate belief they are good with romantic patter. This mistaken impression flows (and the word is used advisedly) from Burns Suppers where renditions of 'My Love Is Like a Red, Red Rose' can persuade monosyllabic men they too possess bard-like wooing charms. Just to relieve everyone from the burden of Burns's romantic legacy, here is an extract of a letter from Rabbie to Clarinda (Agnes McElhose) – the married woman about whom Burns wrote beautiful songs like 'Ae Fond Kiss'.

Now for a little news that will please you. I this morning as I came home, called for a certain woman. I am disgusted with her; I cannot endure her! I, while my heart smote me for the prophanity, tried to compare her with my Clarinda; 'twas setting the expiring glimmer of a farthing taper beside the cloudless glory of the meridian sun. Here was tasteless insipidity, vulgarity of soul and mercenary fawning; there polished good sense, heaven born genius and the most generous, the most delicate, the most tender Passion. I have done with her and she with me.

In fact, six weeks later, Burns married Jean Armour, something he left friends to tell Clarinda. With devious intent behind even great chat-up lines like these, no wonder a gal needs some handy put-downs.

Man: So, wanna go back to my place?
Woman: Well, I don't know. Will two people fit under a rock?

Man: I'd like to call you. What's your number?
Woman: It's in the phone book.
Man: But I don't know your name.
Woman: That's in the phone book too.

Man: So what do you do for a living?
Woman: Female impersonator.

Man: What sign were you born under?
Woman: No Entry.

Man: I like your approach.
Woman: Now let's see your departure.

Bald man : Where have you been all my life?
Young woman: For the first half of it, I wasn't born.

7

GADGETS THEY CAN'T USE

Whatever happened to Scotsmen who once were so hot on the technology front? The men who invented everything from the steam engine to the television are now unable to phone home and they get upset when confronted by the simplest of tasks like loading a washing machine or setting the temperature prior to possibly using an iron. How the mighty are fallen! The West of Scotland male gene pool was once the most productive in the world. Now they're renowned only for being the sick men of Europe and spending more time before the mirror preening than anywhere else in the UK. How did it all go wrong?

The modern male benefits from so many Scots inventions from the past. He uses a car with tyres invented by J B Dunlop from Ayrshire, to drive on tarmac invented by John Loudon McAdam from Ayr, to get to the ferry whose steam engine (OK, not many of them left these days!) was invented by James Watt from Greenock, where he gets out wearing a plastic mackintosh invented by Charles Macintosh from Glasgow, goes below decks to watch TV, invented by John Logie Baird from Helensburgh, and finally calls a mate with a phone invented by Alexander Graham Bell from Edinburgh, to say the ship will only accept English notes made by the Bank of England founded by William Paterson from Dumfries. It is so sad. Seems *looking* big matters more than *thinking* big these days.

Take briefcases – why do men carry them? To put a banana in for lunchtime and to carry something BIGGER than handbags? Let's face it, if the 'modern' west of Scotland man could carry a filing cabinet with steel hub-caps – they would tote these instead.

Come back mild, inventive Victorian men – all is forgiven!

Q. How do you force a man to do sit-ups?
A. Put the remote between his toes.

Q. What's the difference between a man and ET?
A. ET phoned home.

Most men don't do laundry because washing machines don't have remote controls.

If they can put a man on the moon, why can't they put them all there?

The boyfriend

Firstly, keep in mind that Boyfriend 5.0 is an entertainment package, while Husband 1.0 is an operating system. Try entering the command C:\I THOUGHT YOU LOVED ME and download Tears 6.2 to install Guilt 3.0. If all works as designed, Husband 1.0 should then automatically run the applications Jewelry 2.0 and Flowers 3.5. But, remember, overuse can cause Husband 1.0 to default to Grumpy Silence 2.5, Happy Hour 7.0 or Beer 6.1.

Beer 6.1 is a very bad program that will create Snoringloudly.wav files. Whatever you do, DO NOT install Mother-in-law 1.0 or reinstall another Boyfriend program. These are not supported applications and will crash Husband 1.0.

In summary, Husband 1.0 has a limited memory and cannot learn new applications quickly. You might consider additional software to improve memory and performance. I personally recommend Hot Food 3.0 and Lingerie 6.9.

8
BASIC UNFAIRNESS

Men and women are equal, eh? The old days, when women were tried as witches and found innocent if they sank to the bottom of ponds, are over. The modern woman can do everything a man can do — drink too much, own their own flats, have Majorcan holidays with pals, enjoy one-night stands and become girl racers. Until . . . Mr Right appears, domesticity beckons and it's ALL CHANGE. He will become the sole driver – she will become a front-seat stookie. She will become the sole drudge shopper – he will develop speciality purchasing skills, concentrating on those exotic items a girl hasn't got the right chromosomes to buy. Like another power tool, another Rolling Stones compilation CD or a six pack of McEwans.

Guys, we may give up complaining about the basic unfairness of it all but never think we don't notice . . .

Because I'm a man
Because I'm a man, when I lock my keys in the car, I will fiddle with a wire clothes hanger and ignore your suggestions that we call for help until long after hypothermia has set in.

Because I'm a man, when the car isn't running very well, I will lift the bonnet and stare at the engine as if I know what I'm looking at. If another man shows up, one of us will say to the other, 'I used to be able to fix these things but now, with all these computers and everything, I wouldn't know where to start.' We will then drink beer.

Because I'm a man, when I catch a cold I need someone to bring me soup and take care of me while I lie in bed and moan. You never get as sick as I do so, for you, this isn't an issue.

Because I'm a man, I can be relied upon to purchase basic groceries at the store, like milk or bread. I cannot be expected to find exotic items like cumin or tofu. For all I know, these are the same thing. And never, under any circumstances, expect me to pick up anything for which 'feminine hygiene product' is a euphemism.

Because I'm a man, when one of our appliances stops working, I will insist on taking it apart, despite evidence this will cost twice as much once the repair person gets here and has to put it back together.

Because I'm a man, I must hold the television remote control in my hand while I watch TV. If the thing has been misplaced, I may miss a whole show looking for it. Although, one time, I was able to survive by holding a calculator.

Because I'm a man, I don't think we're all that lost and, no, I don't think we should stop and ask someone. Why would you listen to a complete stranger? I mean how the hell could he know where we're going?

Because I'm a man, there is no need to ask me what I'm thinking about. The answer is always either sex or food, though I have to make up something else when you ask – so don't.

Because I'm a man, I do not want to visit your mother or have your mother visit us or talk to her when she calls or think about her any more than I have to. Whatever you got her for Mother's Day is OK – I don't need to see it. And get another one for my mum, too!

Because I'm a man, I am capable of announcing, 'One more beer and I really have to go,' and mean it every single time I say it – even when one bar closes and my mates and I have to hunt another down. I will find it increasingly hilarious to have my pals call you to tell you I'll be home soon and, no, I don't understand why you threw all my clothes into the front garden.

Because I'm a man, you don't have to ask me if I liked the movie. Chances are, if you're crying at the end of it, I didn't.

Because I'm a man, I think what you're wearing is fine. I thought what you were wearing five minutes ago was fine, too. Either pair of shoes is fine. With the belt or without it looks fine. Your hair is fine. You look fine. Can we just go now?

Because I'm a man and this is, after all, the twenty-first century, I will share equally in the housework. You just do the laundry, the cooking, the gardening, the cleaning and the dishes. I'll do the rest.

List of reasons why men are just happier people

Your last name stays put.

The garage is all yours.

You can never be pregnant.

You can wear a white T-shirt to a water park.

You can wear NO T-shirt to a water park.

Car mechanics tell you the truth.

The world is your urinal.

You never have to drive to another petrol station toilet because the first one is just too disgusting.

Same work, more pay.

Wrinkles add character.

People never stare at your chest when you're talking to them.

The occasional well-rendered burp is expected.

One mood – all the time.

Phone conversations are over in thirty seconds flat.

You know things about drains.

A five-day holiday requires only one suitcase.

You can open all your own jars.

You get extra credit for the slightest act of thoughtfulness.

Three pairs of shoes are more than enough.

You are unable to see wrinkles in your clothes.

The same hairstyle lasts for years – maybe even decades.

You only have to shave your face and neck.

You can play with toys all your life.

One wallet, one pair of shoes, one colour for all seasons.

You can wear shorts no matter how your legs look.

You can 'do' your nails with a penknife.

You can do Christmas shopping for twenty-five relatives on 24 December in ten minutes.

9
FOOTBALL OBSESSED

Have you ever considered how many shelves could be fitted, spare rooms decorated, parent-craft courses attended or books written if . . . Scotland's football grounds were closed every other weekend. Never mind windfarms, the collective energy expended twice a week on swearing, dribbling, shouting, singing and crying – not to mention peeing on motorway hard shoulders or staying awake through five hours of drink fuelled post-match analysis – could completely revitalise Scotland. Mind you, these days, it's only the dedicated and the rich who part with the cost of a small family holiday to become season ticket holders and see their team cuffed by Celtic a few times a year.

Instead, most modern footie fanmen are happy to support their team to the death from the Bud-drenched comfort of their girl-friend's sofa – interrupting bursts of invective about the poofy nature of the European male for a quick swatch at the Tuscan Third Division.

Footie fans tolerate being ripped off, patronised, cheated and treated like mugs because . . . well, if you figure it out, tell them.

The Stranded Scotsman

One day, a Scotsman, who has been stranded on a desert island for over ten years, sees an unusual speck on the horizon. 'It's certainly not a ship,' he thinks to himself. As the speck gets closer and closer, he begins to rule out the possibilities of a small boat, then even a raft.

Suddenly, emerging from the surf comes a drop-dead gorgeous blonde woman wearing a wet suit and scuba gear. She approaches the stunned man and says to him, 'Tell me, how long has it been since you've had a cigarette?'

'Ten years,' replies the Scotsman.

With that, she reaches over and unzips a water-proof pocket on her left sleeve and pulls out a pack of fresh cigarettes. He takes one, lights it, takes a long drag and says, 'Jings – that was braw!'

'And how long has it been since you've had a dram?' she asks him.

Trembling, the castaway replies, 'Ten years.'

She reaches over, unzips her right sleeve, pulls out a flask and hands it to him. He opens the flask, takes a long swig and says, 'Oh, my God, absolutely fantastic!'

At this point, she starts slowly unzipping the long zipper that runs down the front of her wet suit and looks at the man. 'And how long has it been since you've played around?' she asks, exposing much of her body.

With tears in his eyes, the man falls to his knees and sobs, 'Oh, Sweet Jesus! Don't tell me you've got a football in there an' aw!'

Q. What's the definition of a Glaswegian pervert?
A. A man who prefers women to football.

Q. What's the definition of a Scottish pervert?
A. A man who prefers women to drink

10
MARRIAGE

Are men worse than women? Or are we as bad as one another? It's amazing how many jokes pop up in both halves of the book. The true horror of finally sleeping with the enemy – marriage – is realising we share many of the same faults and the same battleground – the bathroom. We raise toilets seats or rather we don't because of the hideous sepia tinted quality of the surrounding carpets, walls and enamel. They raise razors. Or they would if a single one remained unblunted by the stubble of countless female hairy bits. But, guys – if you want gals to pretend they are smooth Barbie dolls to contrast with your own Jungle Jim masculinity – live with our razor habits. And don't think you can start a secret stash – you'd have to buy them on your own, right?

Another science bit. Married men live longer than single men – single women live longer than married women. Why? One thing's for sure – any good habits bachelors possess seem to go out the window when they no longer have to sing for their supper (as it were). So watch out complacent, non-flower-wielding anniversary-forgetting husbands – a boring marriage can bring out the vixen in a girl.

Q. What's a man's idea of honesty in a relationship?
A. Telling you his name.

Q. What do men use for birth control?
A. Their personality.

Q. What's the difference between a husband and a vibrator?
A. A vibrator won't make you sleep in the wet patch.

Barbara Walters did a story on gender roles in Kabul several years before the Afghan conflict. She noted that women customarily walked about ten paces behind their husbands. She returned to Kabul recently and observed that the men now walked several paces behind their wives. Ms Walters approached one of the Afghan women and said, 'This is marvellous. Can you tell the free world just what enabled women to achieve this reversal of roles?'

'Land mines,' said the woman.

A man and his wife were having an argument about who should brew the coffee each morning. The wife said, 'You should do it because you get up first and then we don't have to wait as long to get our coffee.'

The husband said, 'You are in charge of cooking around here and you should do it because that is your job and I can just wait for my coffee.'

Wife replies, 'No, you should do it and, besides, it is in the Bible that the man should do the coffee.'

Husband replies, 'I can't believe that. Show me.'

So she fetched the Bible and opened the New Testament at HEBREWS.

Q. What do you call a woman who knows where her husband is every night?
A. A widow.

Q. What do all men at singles bars have in common?
A. They're married.

After the party, as the couple was driving home the woman asks, 'Honey, has anyone ever told you how handsome, sexy and irresistible to women you are?'

The flattered husband says, 'No, dear, they haven't.'

The wife yells, 'Then what the hell gave you THAT idea tonight?'

A man stood over his golf shot for what seemed an age.

His frustrated partner finally said, 'What's taking you so long?'

The man answers, 'My wife is up there watching from the clubhouse – I want to make it the perfect shot.'

'Get real! You haven't a hope in hell of hitting her from here.'

He said, 'I don't know why you wear a bra – you've got nothing to put in it.'

She said, 'You wear trousers don't you?'

He said, 'What have you been doing with all the grocery money I gave you?'

She said, 'Turn sideways and look in the mirror!'

Q. Why are married women heavier than single women?
A. Single women come home, see what's in the fridge and go to bed. Married women come home, see what's in bed and go to the fridge.

For all those men who say, 'Why buy the cow when you can get the milk free,' here's an update for you. Nowadays 80% of women are against marriage. Why? Because women realise it's not worth buying an entire pig just to get a little sausage.

Q. How can you keep your husband truly happy?
A. Who cares?

Q. How many ex-husbands does it take to change a light bulb?
A. Academic – they never seem to keep the house.

Q. How do you stop a lust-filled man?
A. Marry him.

Q. Why do men get married?
A. So they won't have to hold their tummies in anymore.

Q. Why do men marry virgins?
A. So they won't hear criticism.

A man walks up to his wife in the morning and pinches her bum. 'You know, if you firmed this up, we could get rid of your corset.'

It was out of character so she bit her tongue.

The next morning the man woke his wife with a pinch on her left breast. 'You know, if you firmed this up, we could get rid of your bra.'

This was too much. So she rolled over and grabbed his penis. 'And if you firmed this up, we could get rid of the milkman, the gardener and the BT engineer!'

11

REVENGE

Revenge is not a thing I've gone in for. Dealing with awkward blokes at the time of the offence is my preferred method – thereafter out of sight, out of mind. I did manage to make an exception with one newspaper editor I took to court but, since that settlement netted a computer, laser printer and a cuddly toy, I think bygones. The last laird to sue me had to abandon his case and watch land reform triumph in Scotland so, I think we too are quits.

But, chaps, beware. It would seem bygones is NOT the reaction most slighted women choose. Women have obviously had enough of the dumb, hapless victim look. If I was a toilet-seat raiser or a married man at a singles bar, I'd be scared – very scared.

A married couple are driving along a road doing a steady forty miles per hour. The wife is behind the wheel. Her husband suddenly looks across at her and speaks in a clear voice. 'Darling,' he says. 'I know we've been married for twenty years, but I want a divorce.'

The wife says nothing, keeps looking at the road ahead but slowly increases her speed to 45 mph. The husband speaks again. 'I don't want you to try and talk me out of it,' he says, 'because I've been having an affair with your best friend, and she's a far better lover than you are.'

Again the wife stays quiet, but grips the steering wheel more tightly and slowly increases the speed to 55. He pushes his luck. 'I want the house,' he says insistently. Up to 60. 'I want the car, too,' he continues. 65 mph.

'And,' he says, 'I'll have the bank accounts, all the credit cards and the boat.'

The car slowly starts veering towards a massive concrete bridge.

This makes him a wee bit nervous, so he asks her: 'Isn't there anything you want?' The wife at last replies – in a quiet and controlled voice.

'No, I've got everything I need,' she says.

'Oh, really?' he inquires, 'so what have you got?' Just before they slam into the wall at 75 mph, the wife turns to him and smiles . . . 'The airbag.'

Q. What should you do if you see your ex-husband rolling around in pain on the ground?
A. Shoot him again.

Q. How can you tell when a man is well hung?
A. When you can just barely slip your finger in between his neck and the noose.

Q. What does it mean when a man is in your bed gasping for breath and calling your name?
A. You didn't hold the pillow down long enough.

A blonde walks into the Bank of Scotland on the Mound in Edinburgh and asks to see the manager. She says she's going to Hong Kong on business for two weeks and needs to borrow £5,000. The manager says the bank will need some kind of security for the loan so the blonde hands over the keys to a new Ferrari. The car is parked on the street in front of the bank, she has the vehicle registration document and everything checks out. The bank agrees to accept the car as collateral for the loan. The manager and the tellers all enjoy a good laugh at the blonde for using a £200,000 Ferrari as collateral against a £5,000 loan. An employee of the bank then proceeds to drive the Ferrari into the bank's underground garage and parks it there.

Two weeks later, the blonde returns, repays the £5,000 and the interest, which comes to £15.41. The manager says, 'Miss, we are very happy to have had your business and this transaction has worked out very nicely but we are a little puzzled. Why leave us your fabulous car as security?'

The blonde replies, 'Where else in Edinburgh can I park my car for two weeks for only £15.41?'

A couple go on holiday to a fishing resort up north. The husband likes to fish at the crack of dawn. The wife likes to read. One morning the husband returns after several hours of fishing and decides to take a nap. Although not familiar with the area, the wife decides to take the boat out. She motors out a short distance, anchors and continues to read her book. Along comes a game warden in his boat. He pulls up alongside the woman and says, 'Good morning, ma'am. What are you doing?'

'Reading a book,' she replies (thinking, 'Isn't that obvious?').

'You're in a restricted fishing area,' he informs her.

'I'm sorry, Officer, but I'm not fishing, I'm reading.'

'Yes, but you have all the equipment. I'll have to take you in and charge you.'

'If you do that, I'll have to charge you with sexual

assault,' says the woman.

'But I haven't even touched you,' says the game warden.

'That's true,' said the woman, 'but as you say, you have all the equipment.'

Women are like apples – the best ones are at the top of the tree.

Many men don't want to reach for the good ones because they are afraid of falling and getting hurt. Instead, they just get the rotten apples from the ground that aren't as good but easy.

So the apples at the top think something is wrong with them when, in reality, they're amazing. So ladies, you just have to wait for the right man to come along – the one who's brave enough to climb all the way to the top of the tree. And remember – while you're waiting – men are like a fine wine. They start out as grapes and it's up to women to stomp the crap out of them until they turn into something acceptable to have dinner with.

The Secret Service had an opening for an assassin. After all of the background checks, interviews and testing were done, there were three finalists – two men and a woman. For the final test, the Secret Service agents took one of the men to a large metal door and handed him a gun. 'We must know that you will follow your instructions, no matter what the circumstances. Inside this room, you will find your wife sitting in a chair. Kill her!!!'

The man said, 'You can't be serious. I could never shoot my wife!'

'Then you're not the right man for this job.'

The second man was given the same instructions. He took the gun and went into the room. All was quiet for about five minutes. Then the man came out with tears in his eyes. 'I tried but I can't kill my wife.'

The agent said, 'You don't have what it takes. Take your wife and go home.'

Finally, it was the woman's turn. She was told she must kill her husband. She took the gun and went into the room. Shots were heard, one shot after another. They heard screaming, crashing, banging on the walls. After a few minutes all was quiet. The door opened slowly and there stood the woman. She wiped the sweat from her brow and said, 'This gun is loaded with blanks. I had to beat him to death with the chair.'

12
THE MALE COMPETITIVE URGE

The competitive urge is probably fine – but, taken to macho extremes, it does stop men learning from life's little adventures. Why do women surprisingly catch the biggest fish in angling? Simple. They listen to advice and act on it. This is next to impossible for most men because the macho brain sees learning as weakness (especially in public). So if a Scotsman is advised that most salmon hug the bank on a particular beat he MUST ignore it and cast into the centre of the river instead.

The girlie mag *Cosmopolitan* found that 20% of its readers were men and decided to launch 'Cosmo Man' as a supplement. Mistake! *Cosmo* men were secret readers trying to achieve a competitive edge with chicks by reading up on their inner fears and urges. Once 'outed' they wouldn't touch either mag with a bargepole.

With such a vein of underlying stubbornness I've often wondered how men tolerate programmes like the hit TV series, *Queer Eye for a Straight Guy*, which shreds a guy's clothes, hair, record collection and flat décor to reshape him as a babe-friendly dude. Simple. The programme confirms that only gay men understand what women want. Result.

A man is driving up a steep, narrow mountain road. A woman is driving the other way. They pass and the woman yells, 'Pig!'

The man rolls down his window and yells, 'Bitch!' He then goes round the corner and crashes into a large sow in the middle of the road. If only men could listen.

A man picks up a female partner at the golf club.

He wins and she has to fulfil his desires.

She does so – though insists on sex Bill Clinton style.

He's so pleased – even without the cigar – that he asks for a return match and the same thing happens. Next time he insists they have full sex but his partner reveals she is really a man in the process of having a sex change.

'Whatever,' he says 'but you've been playing off the ladies tees!'

Q. How do you stop men reading your emails?
A. Store them in a folder labelled 'Instruction Manuals'.

13
HAVING TO COME FIRST

Let's not forget the other competition-related disorder – having to come first. The old adage about women and children may still apply to sinking ships. But on dry land it's men who push to the front of queues and men who need to be treated first in doctors' surgeries because they are 'in a hurry'. Like women are just meandering through another pointless day, counting our pin-money and planning the next girls' night out.

Another science bit – more women work in Scotland currently than men. Admittedly many work part-time but if anyone thinks the other part is spent sipping Bacardi Breezers and watching live Italian league netball, let me mutter one word. Housework.

Now, in their defence, biologists claim the male ego is a part of the survival instinct. In which case it's a miracle women have survived without one.

But don't worry chaps. When you finally come second absolutely everywhere and not just the classroom, lecture theatre, bedroom and modern workplace, the knitting and nappy changing await you.

We've been keeping second place nice and warm . . .

Three men and a woman are hanging on a rope from a helicopter after a bridge rescue. They know there are too many people on the rope and they'll all die if someone doesn't get off. But they can't decide who should make the sacrifice. Finally the woman gives a really touching speech, talks about giving up things for her husband and children and explains she is used to self-sacrifice – offering things to men and not expecting anything in return. The men are so impressed they all applaud her bravery.

Never underestimate female intelligence.

A man and a woman are in a terrible accident. Both cars are write-offs but, amazingly, neither is hurt. The woman says, 'We are alive. This is a sign from god that we should be friends and live in peace all the rest of our days.'

The man is relieved. 'Oh, yes. Absolute peace.'

The woman goes on, 'And here is a half bottle of whisky. Surely a sign that god wants us to drink to our good fortune.' She hands the bottle to the man.

He drinks half of it and hands it back. She screws the lid back on and puts it in her bag.

The man asks, 'Aren't you having any?'

The woman says, 'Not until the police have arrived.'

On the eighth day God looks down and spots Adam and Eve. He says, 'I've got some leftovers from Creation and can't decide who should get what. The first item is a thing that lets you pee standing up.'

Adam jumps up and yells, 'Mine!'

Eve thinks, 'Damn, I must try to be faster.'

'Oh, well,' says God, 'I'm afraid all I have left is this multiple orgasm.'

Q. How many men does it take to screw in a light bulb?
A. One – he just holds it up there and waits for the world to revolve around him.
OR
A. One to screw in the bulb and two to listen to him brag about the screwing part.

14
INSENSITIVITY

Were men built without feelings or do they train hard to emulate wood, tungsten or granite when faced with anything short of slack-mouthed adulation?

Take the plumber (ladies, we must) who cheerfully announces he must leave an entire family using bottles of water to flush the loo for a weekend that includes the incontinent wean's fifth birthday party. Astonishment, horror, shock, tears, wailing, even dribbling and deep sobs with runny noses all make no impact because . . . it's not his fault if the boss can't schedule the work, lady.

Take the David-Brent-type boss who publicly reveals that his secretary has been wearing incontinence pads for three years to support his claim that disabled people are welcome in the workforce.

In the hit BBC series, *The Office*, the stunned workforce rarely react to each outburst of storm force insensitivity. People – such restraint is unnecessary.

These kind of men can bore on in the face of yawning, pain, disbelief or even small cards with 'Die now' written on them. Do they simply miss these large visual clues or do they realise that other people's feelings will inevitably narrow their own room for manoeuvre?

Either way, ain't it strange that men, who usually can't even communicate with a cat, believe they can negotiate world peace? Or run hospitals . . .

Men seem to think that women make a terrible fuss about easy procedures like having their first mammogram (that's a pap scan boys). So the New Men in charge of the Scottish Health Service have devised a few simple exercises to help the weaker sex prepare. Best of all, shy women can do these exercises in the privacy of their own homes.

EXERCISE 1
Open your refrigerator door and insert one breast between the door and freezer box. Have one of your strongest friends slam the door shut as hard as possible and lean on the door for good measure. Hold that position for five seconds. Repeat.

EXERCISE 2

Visit your garage at 3am when the temperature of the cement floor is perfect. Take off all your clothes and lie comfortably on the floor sideways with one breast wedged under the rear tyre of the car. Ask a friend to slowly reverse the car until your breast is sufficiently flattened and chilled. Switch sides and repeat for the other breast.

EXERCISE 3

Freeze two metal bookends overnight. Strip to the waist and invite a stranger into the room. Have the stranger press the bookends together as hard as they can. Set an appointment with the stranger to do it all over again same time next year!

MENtal illness, MENstrual cramps, MENopause – ever noticed how most of womens problems start with MEN?

A man and his wife were in court getting a divorce. The problem was who should get custody of the child. The wife jumped up and said, 'Your Honour, I brought the child into the world with pain and labour. She should be in my custody.'

The judge turns to the husband and says, 'What do you have to say?'

The man sat for a while contemplating and then slowly rose. 'Your Honour. If I put a pound in a vending machine and a Pepsi comes out, whose Pepsi is it – the machine's or mine?'

One night a woman finds her husband standing over their new sleeping baby. She looks on as his face changes from disbelief to delight, amazement, scepticism and enchantment. Touched by this unusual display of sensitivity and emotion she slips her arms round her husband. 'A penny for your thoughts,' she says.

'I'm just speechless,' the husband replies. 'How anyone could make this cot for £49.99 beats me!'

MEN

VS
WOMEN

**Why Men Are
Better Than Women**

Men start here

IAN BLACK

BLACK & WHITE PUBLISHING

First published 2004
by Black & White Publishing Ltd
99 Giles Street, Edinburgh EH6 6BZ

ISBN 1 84502 021 9

British Library Cataloguing in Publication Data:
A catalogue record for this book is available
from the British Library.

Cover illustration by Bob Dewar

Printed and bound in Denmark by AIT Nørhaven A/S

CONTENTS

MEN vs WOMEN

INTRODUCTION

John Gray, the guy who wrote *Men Are from Mars, Women Are from Venus*, could not have been more wrong than if he had been a woman, and surgery is suspected, not to mention skullduggery. It can now be exclusively revealed, by our extraterrestrial correspondent, ET, who is considered a major beauty among her kind, that men are actually from Earth.

Women, on the other hand, are from a tiny crazed planet the size of a marble in a star system in a galaxy in a meta-galaxy that is so far away that Picard and Kirk have never even dreamed of boldly going within a quintillion parsecs of it. They are utterly alien and they have invaded our peaceful planet, sowing dissention, catastrophe and confusion, by insinuating their slimy miniscule virus-sized bodies into our females and creating a low type of cunning thinking, teetering almost on the edge of intelligence, that never existed before their arrival.

Think about it, chaps. As far as females go, there are dogs, horses and budgies that are easier to under-

stand. You speak, they hear you, they respond. In fact, there are giant turtles, jellyfish and bacteria that are easier to communicate with than females, and who are less confusing when they do respond. Bricks too. You never get an argument from a brick.

Help is at hand, though, as research has established that we are beginning to develop defences. These wo-men, as they call themselves (what an obvious clue. They must think that we are really dumb), are allergic to testosterone and are repelled by the smell of huge quantities of beer on the breath. The former testosterone factories like Hampden and Murrayfield may have been infiltrated by them in recent years, as results indicate, but there are still huge motorbikes to be purchased with the retirement fund, beer to be bought and darts and snooker to be shouted at on the telly.

Your sex needs you, just as you need your sex.

Welcome back to the fight.

1
DIFFERENT DRIVERS

All men know that women can't drive properly – we just don't talk about it much. Here are a couple of examples of why they should learn.

A married couple are driving along a motorway doing 60 mph, the husband behind the wheel. His wife suddenly looks over at him and says: "Darling, I know we've been married for twenty years, but I want a divorce." The husband says nothing but slowly increases his speed to 70 mph. She then says: "I don't want you to try and talk me out of it, because I've been having an affair with your best friend, and he's a lot better at sex than you."

Again the husband stays quiet but speeds up more as his anger increases. "I want the house," she insists, pushing her luck.

Again the husband speeds up, now to 80 mph. She says: "I want the car too!" but he just keeps driving faster and faster.

By now he's up to 90 mph. "And I want the bank

7

accounts and all the credit cards." The husband starts to veer towards the central reservation. This makes her a little nervous so she asks hesitantly: "Isn't there anything you want, dear?"

The husband replies: "No, I've got everything I need, darling."

"Oh really," she says, "so what have you got?" Just before they smash into the central reservation at 100 mph, the husband smiles and says:

"The airbag!"

Driving to the office this morning on the motorway, I looked over to my right and there was a man in a brand new BMW (obviously) . . . doing 90 mph, with his face up close to the rear view mirror, shaving!

I looked away for a couple of seconds and when I looked back he was halfway over in my lane still working on the face fuzz!

It scared me (I am a woman) so much so that I dropped my mascara brush, which knocked the bacon roll out of my other hand.

In the confusion of trying to straighten out the car using my knees against the steering wheel, I knocked the mobile phone from my ear and it fell into the coffee between my legs, which splashed and burned, making me scream, which allowed the cigarette to fall out my mouth, ruined my blouse

AND disconnected an important call!
Fucking men drivers!

2
THE DATING GAME: SOME DEFINITIONS

Every man knows that dating was invented by women as a means of getting free food and drink from as many men as possible before picking the richest one to have occasional sex with.

Dating Terms

DATING
The process of spending enormous amounts of money, time and energy to get better acquainted with a person whom you don't especially like in the present and will learn to like a lot less in the future.

EASY
A term used to describe a woman who has the morals of a man.

EYE CONTACT
A method utilised by a single woman to communicate to a man that she is interested in him. Despite being advised to do so, many women have difficulty looking a man directly in the eyes, not necessarily due to shyness, but usually due to the fact that a woman's eyes are not located in her chest.

FRIEND
A member of the opposite sex of your acquaintance who has some flaw which makes sleeping with him/her totally unappealing.

INDIFFERENCE
A woman's feeling towards a man, which is interpreted by the man as "playing hard to get".

IRRITATING HABIT
What the endearing little qualities that initially attract two people to each other turn into after a few months together.

NYMPHOMANIAC
A man's term for a woman who wants to do it more often than he does.

SOBER
A condition in which it is almost impossible to fall in love.

ATTRACTION
The act of associating horniness with a particular person.

LOVE AT FIRST SIGHT
What occurs when two extremely horny but not entirely choosy people meet.

LAW OF RELATIVITY
How attractive a given person appears to be is directly proportionate to how unattractive your date is.

3
TWO SIDES TO EVERY STORY

We all know about the phases of the moon affecting women's behaviour but what, apart from a paucity of sex, is it that makes men moody?

Her side of the story . . .

"He was in an odd mood on Sunday night. We planned to meet at the pub for a quick drink. I spent the afternoon shopping with the girls and I thought it might have been my fault because I was a bit later than I'd promised. He didn't say anything about it. The conversation was very slow so I thought we should go somewhere more intimate and talk privately. We went to a nice restaurant and he was STILL acting a bit funny. I tried to cheer him up. I started to wonder whether it was me or something else. I asked him and he said no. I wasn't really sure. In the taxi on the way home, I said I loved him deeply. He just put his arm around me. I didn't know what the hell that meant because he didn't say it back. We finally got home and I was wondering if

he was going to leave me! So I tried to get him to talk but he just switched on the TV. Reluctantly I said I was going to bed. After about ten minutes, he joined me. To my surprise, we made love. He still seemed really incredibly distracted though. Afterwards, I just wanted to confront him, but I cried myself to sleep. I just don't know what to do any more. I really think he is seeing someone else".

His side of the story . . .

"Motherwell lost again. Got a shag though."

4

A COCK AND BULL STORY

Familiarity, as we know, breeds contempt but usually fails to breed anything else, which is why sperm donors are given different magazines each time. OK, OK, I made that up. I don't know if they do or not. Here's a wee story about familiarity, contempt and breeding.

A man takes his wife to the Highland Show. They start walking down the row of pens that have the bulls. They come up to the first bull and his sign says: "This bull mated 50 times last year." The wife turns to her husband and says: "He mated 50 times in a year. You could learn from him."

They proceed to the next bull and his sign says: "This bull mated 65 times last year." The wife says: "This one mated 65 times last year. That is over 5 times a month. You can learn from this one too." They proceed to the last bull and his sign says: "This bull mated 365 times last year." The wife's mouth

drops open and she says: "Goodness. He mated 365 times last year. That's once a day! You could really learn from this one."

The man turns to his wife and says: "Go up and ask if it was 365 times with the same cow."

5
A SCOTTISH VALENTINE

You've got to be romantic, haven't you, lads? Particularly on this day. Don't forget now. It could mean no sex for a while. As someone who absent-mindedly signed a passionate card "Ian Black", I know whereof I speak.

Of course I love ye darling . . .
You're a stoatin' top notch burd
And when I say you're gorgeous
I mean every single word
So yer bum is on the big side
I don't mind a bit of flab
It means that when I'm ready
There's something there to grab

So your tummy isn't as flat as it was
I'm telling ye, I don't care
so long as when I cuddle ye
I can get my arms around there

I swear on ma granny's grave now
The moment that we met
I thought you were as good as
I was ever gonny get
No matter what ye look like
I'll always love ye dear
Now shut up while the fitba's on
And get me another beer!

6
GENDER ISSUES

OK, chaps and chapesses, here's a challenge. Chaps, you have to explain to your lady why you pee outside a lot without mentioning the words: "Because I can," and girls, you have to keep that sneery little moue of disgust off your face, the one that every single woman in the world produces when this subject comes up. Knew you couldn't, girls. We guys know you've all done it too and we don't sneer, so what is the problem here? Oh yes, it's a gender issue. Pun intended.

From the *Washington Post* Style Invitation, in which it was postulated that English should have male and female nouns. Readers were asked to assign a gender to nouns of their choice and explain their reasons. Here are some of them:

SWISS ARMY KNIFE – male. Even though it appears useful for a wide variety of work, it spends most of its time just opening bottles.

TYRE – male. It goes bald and is often over-inflated.

HOT AIR BALLOON – male. To get it to go anywhere, you have to light a fire under it.

SPONGES – female. They are soft and squeezable and they retain water.

WEB PAGE – female. It is always getting hit on.

SHOE – male. It is usually unpolished, with its tongue hanging out.

COPIER – female. Once turned off, it takes a while to warm up. It is an effective reproductive device when the right buttons are pushed. And it can wreak havoc when the wrong buttons are pushed.

ZIPLOC BAGS – male. They hold everything in, but you can always see right through them.

SUBWAY – male. It uses the same old lines to pick up people.

HOURGLASS – female. Over time, the weight shifts to the bottom.

HAMMER – male. It hasn't evolved much over the last 5,000 years but it's handy to have around.

REMOTE CONTROL – female. Ha! . . . you thought it would be male. But consider this: it gives man pleasure; he'd be lost without it; and, while he doesn't always know the right buttons to push, he keeps trying and trying and trying!

7
SAYING THE RIGHT THING

Been there, done this, already using the T-shirt as a beer mopper. It's incredibly difficult to train your subconcious to lie but they teach us boys it at school. That PE stuff is a front, girls.

Willie wakes up at home with a huge hangover. He forces himself to open his eyes and the first thing he sees is a couple of Alka Seltzer and a glass of water on the side table. He sits down and sees his clothes in front of him, all clean and pressed. He looks around the room and sees that it is in a perfect order, spotlessly clean. And so is the rest of the house.

He takes the Alka Seltzer and notices a note on the table: "Breakfast is in the oven. Love you."

So he goes to the kitchen and sure enough there is a hot breakfast, orange juice, toast, fresh newspaper, the works. His son is also at the table, eating.

Father: "Son, what happened yesterday?"

Son: "Oh, the usual. You came home after 3 am, drunk and delirious. Broke some furniture and threw up in the hall."

Father: "So, why is everything so clean and tidy and the food on the table?"

Son: "Oh, that! Mum dragged you to the bedroom, and when she tried to take your trousers off you said: 'Leave me alone, woman. I'm married!'"

8
HOW TO BE POLITICALLY CORRECT WITH WOMEN

It is impossible for men to be politically correct with men, particularly if they know you, and you know the reason that we are PC with you, don't you ladies? Yep, same reason that we talk to you at all, another being the fact that sheep can't operate keyboards. So, always remember that:

She is not a BLEACHED BLONDE
She is PEROXIDE DEPENDENT

She is not a BAD COOK
She is MICROWAVE COMPATIBLE

She does not wear TOO MUCH JEWELLERY
She is METALLICALLY OVERBURDENED

She is not CONCEITED
She is INTIMATELY AWARE OF HER
BEST QUALITIES

She does not want to be MARRIED
She wants to lock you in DOMESTIC INCARCER-
ATION

She does not GAIN WEIGHT
She is a METABOLIC UNDERACHIEVER

She does not TEASE or FLIRT
She engages in ARTIFICIAL STIMULATION

She is not STUPID
She is a DETOUR OFF THE INFORMATION SUPER-
HIGHWAY

She is not TOO THIN
She is SKELETALLY PROMINENT

She does not HAVE A MOUSTACHE
She is IN TOUCH WITH HER MASCULINE SIDE

She does not HATE TELEVISED SPORT
She is ATHLETICALLY IGNORANT

She has not BEEN AROUND A BIT
She is a PREVIOUSLY ENJOYED COMPANION

She does not WEAR TOO MUCH PERFUME
She commits FRAGRANCE ABUSE

She does not GO SHOPPING
She is PURCHASING FLUENT

She is not an AIRHEAD
She is REALITY IMPAIRED

She does not get DRUNK or TIPSY
She gets CHEMICALLY INCONVENIENCED

She does not get FAT or CHUBBY
She achieves MAXIMUM DENSITY

She is not COLD or FRIGID
She is THERMALLY INACCESSIBLE

She does not WEAR TOO MUCH MAKEUP
She has reached COSMETIC SATURATION

She does not NAG
She becomes VERBALLY REPETITIVE

9
THE PERFECT COUPLE

As Joe E. Brown so memorably said at the end of *Some Like It Hot*: "Well, nobody's perfect". Lots of women act as if perfection isn't good enough. Here's one of them.

Once upon a time, a perfect man and a perfect woman met. After a perfect courtship, they had a perfect wedding. Their life together was, of course, perfect. One snowy, stormy Christmas Eve, this perfect couple was driving their perfect car (a British racing green Jag) along a winding road, when they noticed someone at the side of the road in distress. Being the perfect couple, they stopped to help. There stood Santa Claus with a huge bundle of toys. Not wanting to disappoint any children on the eve of Christmas, the perfect couple loaded Santa and his toys into their car. Soon they were driving along delivering toys. Unfortunately, the driving conditions deteriorated and the perfect couple and Santa Claus

had an accident. Only one of them survived the accident.

The mind-numbing question is: Who was the survivor?

Think about it. The answer's obvious, really . . .

The perfect woman survived. She's the only one who really existed in the first place. Everyone knows there is no Santa Claus and there is no such thing as a perfect man. Women, stop reading here. That is the end of the joke.

Men, keep on reading . . .

So, if there is no perfect man and no Santa Claus, the perfect woman must have been driving. And that explains why there was an accident. By the way, if you're a woman and you're reading this, this illustrates another point: Women never listen, either.

10
ADVICE

OK, guys, hands up anyone who has ever taken and acted upon a piece of advice offered by a partner. Not a lot of hands up, eh? But you do take it from your mates because it is useful stuff, like: "Put it to the back post in front of Tommy, he's got the beating of that back in the air", not: "We should talk more", and stuff like that. Hands up again guys, have any of you ever said, or had said to you by a mate: "We should talk more"? Not too many hands again this time. Here is some useful advice.

If your wife is fat, make her walk ten miles a day. In a month's time, she'll be 300 miles away.

How do you know when it's time to wash the dishes and clean up the house?
    Look inside your trousers. If you have a penis, it's not time.

1. It is important to find a woman who helps at home, who cooks from time to time, cleans up and has a job.
2. It is important to find a woman who can make you laugh.
3. It is important to find a woman you can trust and who doesn't lie to you.
4. It is important to find a woman who is good in bed and who likes to be with you.
5. It is very important that these four women don't know each other.

Words to live by:
Do not argue with a spouse who is packing your parachute.

Every man knows that there are days in the month when all a man has to do is open his mouth and he takes his life in his hands. This is a handy guide that should be in the wallet of every husband, boyfriend or significant other.

DANGEROUS: What's for dinner?
SAFER: Can I help you with dinner?
SAFEST: Where would you like to go for dinner?

DANGEROUS: Are you wearing THAT?
SAFER: Goodness, you look good in brown.
SAFEST: Superb! Look at you!

DANGEROUS: What are you so worked up about?
SAFER: Could we be overreacting?
SAFEST: Here's fifty quid.

DANGEROUS: Should you be eating that?
SAFER: You know, there are a lot of apples left.
SAFEST: Can I get you a glass of wine with that?

DANGEROUS: What did you DO all day?
SAFER: I hope you didn't overdo it today.
SAFEST: I've always loved you in that dressing gown.

11
FOUR LETTER WORDS

Some four letter words retain their power, like 'mana' for instance, and some have lost theirs through overuse. Here are a few that still have the power to disturb.

A young couple got married and left on their honeymoon. When they got back, the bride immediately called her mother.

"Well, how was the honeymoon?" asked the mother.

"Oh, Mum," she replied, "the honeymoon was wonderful! So romantic . . ." Suddenly she burst out crying. "But, Mum, as soon as we returned, Tam started using the most horrible language. He's been saying things I've never heard before. All these awful four-letter words! You've got to come and get me and take me home . . . please Mum."

"Calm down, Jeannie," her mother said. "Calm down. Tell me, what could be so awful? What four-letter words has he been using?"

"Please don't make me tell you, Mum," wept the daughter, "I'm so embarrassed. They're just too awful. You've got to come and get me and take me home . . . please Mum!"

"Darling, you must tell me what has you so upset. Be brave. Tell your mother these horrible four-letter words."

Still sobbing, the bride replied, "Oh, Mum . . . words like cook, dust, wash, and iron . . ."

12
FREEDOM AND FUN GUARANTEED

This is the only joke in this section about men being dumb and menstruation. See me, see restrained?

Two Glasgow men saved up all year and went to Blackpool for a week for their holidays. They had a wild time gorging themselves on pink rock and milk stout and running around in Kiss-Me-Quick hats playing all the video machines and spending their nights in pubs.

Such a wild time, in fact, that by the Friday they only had a quid between them and a whole day to spend before the coach left for Glasgow that night.

"Tell you what," says one to the other, "take the quid and go down to the shops and buy a pack of cards or something to keep us amused. It'll give us something to do."

So his mate goes down to the shops and comes back five minutes later with a packet of Tampax.

"What the hell did you get these for?" asks the first guy.

"Well," says his mate, "look at the side of the packet. It says we can go swimming, or horse-riding, or play tennis, lots of activities."

13
WOMEN'S QUESTIONS ANSWERED

1. WHY ARE MEN SUCH PRICKS?
It's a testosterone thing. In a similar way to your
PMT thing, we men suffer from testosterone
poisoning. Why do you think the average life span of
a male is typically ten years shorter (and it's not just
from all the bitching and nagging we have to
endure)? Hormones modify behaviour. We're just
misunderstood.

*2. WHY DO MEN ALWAYS HAVE TO OGLE
AT OTHER WOMEN?*
Again, this is a testosterone thing. Do you honestly
think that all the testosterone just fell out of our
bodies the moment we met you? Besides, women do
it as well. Women are just much better at not getting
caught. I'm fairly certain it's some sort of photo-
graphic memory deal. Women take one quick look
and memorise it for later reference. Since men lack

this ability, we try to burn it into our memory by staring as much as we can.

3. WHY DO MEN ALWAYS TOUCH THEMSELVES, ESPECIALLY IN PUBLIC?

We occasionally need to adjust our little friend and make him happy. It's much like adjusting your bra. Being in public is just an added bonus.

4. WHY DO MEN ALWAYS SAY SUCH STUPID THINGS?

We like to. It's actually a whole lot of fun to see our partners frustrated by a few simple (and well-chosen) words.

5. WHY ARE MEN SO UNCOMMUNICATIVE?

You'd learn to keep your big mouth shut too if every time you open it you get into trouble with your partner.

6. WHY DO MEN HAVE TO ACT LIKE SUCH IDIOTS?

Well, we don't actually have to – we do it because we enjoy it. It's the old-fashioned pride in a job well done that's missing in so much of the world now-adays.

7. WHY CAN'T MEN JUST SHARE THEIR FEELINGS?

Do we look like women to you? Why is it so hard to understand that men and women are different? How are we supposed to share how we feel when we have no idea how we feel? Unless we're experiencing some extreme emotion like rage, hatred, disgust or a brick on our foot, we have no idea how we feel. Personally, I get a headache whenever I try to figure out how I feel.

8. WHY CAN'T MEN CUDDLE MORE (ie, LIE DOWN AND HUG)?

Please . . . How many hours do you think there are in a day? We oblige you as much as we can, but who the hell (besides women) can stand lying around for hours on end? We men . . . Men hunters . . . Need go roam . . . Starve in cave . . . Must go find wildebeest . . . Now, on the other hand, sitting on our arses for hours on end is a whole other story.

9. HOW CAN MEN SIT ON THEIR ARSES ALL DAY WITHOUT MOVING?

Men have very powerful sets of sitting muscles developed by evolution that enable us to sit for extended periods of time without getting tired. In prehistoric times, it was often necessary to sit in one

spot for extended periods of time while hunting for prey. The more successful hunters were able to sit very still for very extended periods of time thereby passing on this ability to their progeny. The fidgety types were all gobbled up by sabre toothed tigers etc. The end result is that almost all modern men are born with this innate ability.

10. WHY CAN'T MEN JUST SAY "I LOVE YOU"?

Men are taught from a tender young age to be self-sufficient. To say that we love you is equivalent to saying that we need you. Most men consider that a character fault. It's not easy to admit to one's own character faults.

11. WHY DO MEN SAY "I LOVE YOU" WHEN THEY HARDLY KNOW ME?

Ho, ho, ho . . . Aren't you special? Well, some men think it's a sure fire way to get into your knickers. Surprisingly, it actually still works quite well.

12. WHY DOESN'T MY PARTNER EVER ANSWER ME?

We just simply don't have the energy to answer every single one of your questions. If we think we do not have the answer, or that you will not like the

answer, we simply remain quiet and save the energy for other things.

13. WHY WON'T MEN EVER TIDY UP AFTER THEMSELVES?

Why should we? It doesn't really bother us that much. Besides, we're pretty sure you'll do it.

14. WHAT'S WITH ALL THE BELCHING AND FARTING?

This usually only occurs after months of courting. It's our way to let you know that we're comfortable with you. Believe it or not, it's actually a sign of affection. Besides, holding it for extended periods of time gives us stomach cramps.

15. WHY DO MEN HATE SHOPPING?

It's an evolutionary thing. Men hunt. Women gather. We just want to go out, kill it and bring it back. Who wants to spend hours and hours looking at things we have no intention of killing? Err . . . buying?

14
WHY FOOTBALL GROUNDS ARE LIKE WOMEN

1. There is a vast difference in grounds with regards to length and width, thus varying the quality of play.
2. Pitches vary from the well grassed to the completely bald.
3. Remember, it is possible to score at both ends.
4. Tackling from behind is not always an offence, check with ground owner.
5. Be careful as, after a few pints, a ground appears to be of premiership standard, but in reality would not even be eligible as a council dumping ground.
6. Only some grounds offer five-a-side facilities.
7. Don't ever make public your desires to play at Hampden. Also, never mention pitches previously visited.

8. Extra time is dependent on subsequent pitch bookings.

9. If the ground does not seem to have undersoil heating, suggest calling the game off, possibly even contact an undertaker.

10. Always look for a ground that has never been played on before (or at least hasn't had many visits). That said, well-used grounds may have better facilities and will really know how to get the best out of a player.

11. Wet pitches allow for long sliding tackles.

12. Always ask before leaving the pitch and entering the tunnel. Do not expect to be allowed to come straight from the tunnel to the goal mouth and score. That can leave an awful taste in the mouth of the pitch owner and may prevent further use of the ground.

13. Personal morals may be compromised by local derbies.

14. From time to time the goal may be obstructed by a highly absorbent goalie.

15. Bulgarian grounds are frequently more grassy.

16. French grounds are frequently very nice to look at, however there can be sometimes an awful smell from the terraces which don't get hosed down as often as they should.

17. Very few grounds are found with executive boxes.

18. Be wary of grounds with room for coaches.

19. Always be on the lookout for grounds that host ladies' footy two evenings a week.

20. Pitches with a soggy end can be out of bounds for up to 5 days a month, although this can be longer if you piss the owner off by continually asking to play up the good end instead.

21. Players must agree personal terms with the club before being allowed to play on the turf.

15
MEN'S RULES OF LIFE

Life has many rules. Here are some of the lesser known ones that all men live by. And I mean all of us.

1. Any man who brings a camera to a stag night may be legally killed.
2. Under no circumstances may two men share an umbrella.
3. It is OK for a man to cry under the following circumstances:
   a. When a heroic dog dies to save its master
   b. The moment Angelina Jolie starts unbuttoning her blouse
   c. After crashing your boss's car
   d. One hour, 12 minutes, 37 seconds into *The Crying Game*
   e. When she is using her teeth.
4. Unless he murdered someone in your family, you must bail a friend out of jail within 12 hours.
5. If you've known a bloke for more than 24 hours,

his sister is off limits for ever, unless you actually marry her.

6. Moaning about the brand of free beer in a mate's fridge is forbidden. Complain at will if the temperature is unsuitable.

7. No man will ever be required to buy a birthday present for another man. In fact, even remembering your mate's birthday is strictly optional.

8. On a trip, the strongest bladder determines stops, not the weakest.

9. When stumbling upon other blokes watching a sporting event, you may ask the score of the game in progress, but you may never ask who's playing.

10. You may flatulate in front of a woman only after you have brought her to climax. If you trap her head under the covers for the purpose of flatulent entertainment, she's officially your girlfriend.

11. It is permissible to quaff a fruity alcopop drink only when you're sunning yourself on a tropical beach . . . and it's delivered by a topless supermodel . . . and it's free.

12. Only in situations of moral and/or physical peril are you allowed to kick another bloke in the nuts.

13. Unless you're in prison, never fight naked.

14. Friends don't let friends wear Speedos. Ever. Issue closed.

15. If a man's fly is down, that's his problem, you didn't see anything.
16. Women who claim they "love to watch sport" must be treated as spies until they demonstrate knowledge of the game and the ability to drink as much as the other sport watchers.
17. You must offer heartfelt and public condolences over the death of a girlfriend's cat, even if it was you who secretly set it on fire and threw it into a fan.
18. A man in the company of a hot, suggestively dressed woman must remain sober enough to fight.
19. Never hesitate to reach for the last beer or the last slice of pizza, but not both.
20. If you compliment a bloke on his six-pack, you'd better be talking about his choice of beer.
21. Never join your girlfriend or wife in dissing a mate of yours, except if she's withholding sex pending your response.
22. Phrases that may not be uttered to another man while lifting weights:
    a. Yeah, baby, push it!
    b. C'mon, give me one more! Harder!
    c. Another set and we can hit the showers!
23. Never talk to a man in a toilet unless you are on equal footing: Both urinating, both queuing, etc.

For all other situations, an almost imperceptible nod is all the conversation you need.

24. Never allow a telephone conversation with a woman to go on longer than you are able to have sex with her. Keep a stopwatch by the phone. Hang up if necessary.

25. You cannot grass on a colleague who shows up at work with a massive hangover. You may however, hide the aspirin, smear his chair with cheese, turn the brightness dial all the way down so he thinks his monitor is broken, and have him paged over the Tannoy every seven minutes.

26. The morning after you and a girl who was formerly "just a friend" have carnal drunken monkey sex, the fact that you're feeling weird and guilty is no reason not to have her again before the discussion about what a big mistake it was.

27. It is acceptable for you to drive her car. It is not acceptable for her to drive yours.

28. Thou shalt not buy a car with an engine capacity of less than 1.5 litres. Thou shall not really buy a car with less than 1.8 litres, 16 valves and a turbo.

29. Thou shalt not buy a car in the colours of brown, pink, lime green, orange or sky blue.

30. The girl who replies to the question "What do

you want for Christmas?" with "If you loved me, you'd know what I want!" gets a Playstation 2.

16
SOME QUOTES

My wife and I were happy for twenty years.
Then we met.

A good wife always forgives her husband
when she's wrong.

I was married by a judge.
I should have asked for a jury.

I bought my wife a new car. She called and said,
"There's water in the carburettor." I asked her, "Where's
the car?" She replied, "In the loch."

The secret of a happy marriage remains a secret.

And, from Phyllis Diller, definitive advice:
"Never go to bed angry. Stay up and fight."

17
SEE MISOGYNY? SEE THIS CHAPTER?

It really should be called misterogyny, shouldn't it?

After a quarrel, a wife said to her husband, "You know, I was a fool when I married you." The husband replied, "Yes, dear, but I was in love and didn't notice."

When a man steals your wife, there is no better revenge than to let him keep her.

I haven't spoken to my wife in 18 months – I don't like to interrupt her.

My girlfriend told me I should be more affectionate. So I got myself two girlfriends.

A man said his credit card was stolen but he decided not to report it since the thief was spending much less than his wife did.

Getting married is very much like going to a restaurant with friends. You order what you want, then when you see what the other fellow has, you wish you had ordered that.

Man is incomplete until he is married. Then he is finished.

A little boy asked his father, "Daddy, how much does it cost to get married?" The father replied, "I don't know son, I'm still paying."

Young son: "Is it true, Dad, that in some parts of Africa a man doesn't know his wife until he marries her?" Dad: "That happens in every country, son."

Then there was a man who said, "I never knew what real happiness was until I got married – then it was too late."

A man placed an advert in the classifieds: "Wife wanted." The next day he received a hundred letters. They all said the same: "You can have mine."

A woman was telling her friend, "I made my husband a millionaire." "And what was he before you married him?" asked the friend. "A billionaire." she replied.

The trouble with being the best man at a wedding is that you never get to prove it.

A man, upon his engagement, went to his father and said, "Dad! I've found a woman just like mother." His father replied, "So what do you want? Sympathy?"

Wise words of Oscar Wilde:
Marriage is the triumph of imagination over intelligence. Second marriage is the triumph of hope over experience.

If you want your wife to listen and pay strict attention to every word you say, talk in your sleep.

It's not true that married men live longer than single men. It only seems longer.

Losing a wife can be very hard. In my case, it was almost impossible.

A man was complaining to a friend: "I had it all – money, a beautiful house, a big car, the love of a beautiful woman – and then, BAM!, it was all gone!" "What happened?" asked his friend. "My wife found out."

Just think, if it weren't for marriage, men would go through life thinking they had no faults at all.

One of the greatest things about marriage is that, as both husband and father, you can say anything you want to around the house. Of course, no one pays the least bit of attention.

A successful man is one who makes more money than his wife can spend. A successful woman is one who can find such a man.

A man meets a genie. The genie tells him he can ask for whatever he wants and he will get it, but his mother-in-law will also get double what he gets. The man thinks for a moment and says, "OK, give me ten million pounds and kick me half to death."

How many men does it take to open a beer? None, it should be opened by the time she brings it.

How do you fix a woman's watch? You don't. There's a clock on the cooker.

Why do men fart more than women? Because women won't shut up long enough to build up pressure.

If your dog is barking at the back door and your wife is yelling at the front door, who do you let in first? The dog of course . . . at least he'll shut up after you let him in.

All wives are alike, but they have different faces so you can tell them apart.

I married Miss Right. I just didn't know her first name was Always.

What do you call a woman who has lost 95% of her intelligence? Divorced.

Bigamy is having one wife too many. Some say monogamy is the same.

Scientists have discovered a food that diminishes a woman's sex drive by 90% . . . Wedding cake.

Marriage is a 3-ring circus: Engagement ring, wedding ring and suffer-ring.

The last fight was my fault. My wife asked, "What's on the TV?" I said, "Dust!"

In the beginning, God created earth and rested.

Then God created man and rested. Then God created woman. Since then, neither God nor man has rested.

My wife and I are inseparable. In fact, last week it took four policemen and a dog.

Why do men die before their wives? They want to.

What is the difference between a dog and a fox? About 5 drinks.

A beggar walked up to a well-dressed woman shopping in Princes Street and said, "I haven't eaten anything in four days." She looked at him and said, "Goodness, I wish I had your willpower."

Do you know the punishment for bigamy? Two mothers-in-law.

First man (proudly): "My wife's an angel!"
Second guy: "You're lucky, mine's still alive."

Men who have pierced ears are better prepared for marriage. They've experienced pain and bought jewellery.

How do most men define marriage? An expensive way to get your laundry done for free.

The most effective way to remember your wife's birthday is to forget once.

18
A WOMAN'S GUIDE TO MALE ENGLISH

Some women think that men are obsessed with having sex. They are right, but it is a genetic thing. You are doing it because your dad did it before you were born.

Some simple man talk:
  I'm hungry = I'm hungry.
  I'm sleepy = I'm sleepy.
  I'm tired = I'm tired.
  Do you want to go to a movie = I'd eventually like to have sex with you.
  Can I take you out to dinner? = I'd eventually like to have sex with you.
  Can I ring you sometime? = I'd eventually like to have sex with you.
  May I have this dance? = I'd eventually like to have sex with you.
  Nice dress = nice tits.

You look tense, let me give you a massage =
I want to fondle you.

What's wrong? = I don't see why you're making
such a big deal out of this.

What's wrong? = what meaningless, self-inflicted
psychological trauma are you going through
now?

What's wrong? = I guess sex tonight is out of the
question.

I'm bored = do you want to have sex?

I love you = let's have sex now.

I love you, too = OK, I said it . . . we'd better have
sex now!

Yes, I like the way you cut your hair = I liked it
better before.

Yes, I like the way you cut your hair = £50 and it
doesn't look that much different!

Let's talk = I am trying to impress you by showing
that I am a deep person and maybe then you'd
like to have sex with me.

Will you marry me? = I want to make it illegal for
other men to have sex with you.

I like that one better (while shopping) = Pick any
bloody dress and let's go home.

19
SEVERAL THINGS THAT YOU WON'T HEAR WOMEN SAY OFTEN

I could write a book about the things that women don't say very often, starting off with: "No, no, it's my round. I'll get this one." Here are some more.

That was fun. When will all your friends be over to watch porn movies again?

You know, I've been complaining a lot lately. I don't blame you for ignoring me.

The new girl in my office is a stripper. I invited her over for dinner on Friday.

I liked that wedding even more than ours. Your ex-girlfriend has style.

That girl is wearing the same outfit as I am. Cool, I'm going to go over and talk to her.

I love hearing stories about your old girlfriends – tell me more.

I like using this new lawnmower so much more than the old one. What a wonderful Valentine's day!

Let's just leave the toilet seat up at all times, then you don't have to bother with it any more.

I'm so happy with my new hairstyle, I don't think I'll ever change it again.

You passed out before brushing your teeth again, you big silly.

You are so much cleverer than my father.

20
WOMEN'S VOCABULARY

Well, chaps, now it can be revealed. Women do do one word answers, but you are not going to like them.

FINE
This is the word women use to end an argument when they feel they are right and you need to shut up. Never use "Fine" to describe how a woman looks – this will cause you to have one of those arguments.

FIVE MINUTES
This is half an hour. It is equivalent to the five minutes that the football is going to last before you take out the rubbish, so it's an even swop.

NOTHING
This means: "something" and you should be on your toes. "Nothing" is usually used to describe the feeling a woman has of wanting to turn you inside out,

upside down, and backwards. "Nothing" usually signifies an argument that will last "Five Minutes" and end with: "Fine".

GO AHEAD (With Raised Eyebrows!)
This is a dare. One that will result in a woman getting upset over "Nothing" and will end with the word "Fine".

GO AHEAD (Normal Eyebrows)
This means: "I give up" or: "Do what you want because I don't care". You will get a "Raised Eyebrow Go Ahead" in just a few minutes, followed by "Nothing" and "Fine" and she will talk to you in about "Five Minutes" when she calms down.

LOUD SIGH
A "Loud Sigh" means she thinks you are an idiot at that moment, and wonders why she is wasting her time standing here and arguing with you over "Nothing".

SOFT SIGH
Again, not a word, but a non-verbal statement. "Soft Sighs" means that she is content. Your best bet is not to move or breathe, and she will stay content.

THAT'S ALL RIGHT

This is one of the most dangerous statements that a woman can make to a man. "That's All Right" means that she wants to think long and hard before paying you back for whatever it is that you have done. "That's All Right" is often used with the word "Fine" and in conjunction with a "Raised Eyebrow".

GO AHEAD

At some point in the near future, you are going to be in big trouble.

PLEASE DO

This is not a statement, it is an offer. A woman is giving you the chance to come up with whatever excuse or reason you have for doing whatever it is that you have done. You have a fair chance with the truth, so be careful and you shouldn't get a "That's All Right".

THANKS

A woman is thanking you. Do not faint. Just say, "No problem."

THANKS A LOT

This is much different from: "Thanks". A woman will say "Thanks A Lot" when she is really pissed off

with you. It signifies that you have offended her in some callous way and will be followed by the "Loud Sigh". Be careful not to ask what is wrong after the "Loud Sigh", as she will only tell you: "Nothing."

21

A DAY IN THE GARDEN OF EDEN

Here's an imaginary conversation, much like the insomniac agnostic dyslexic, who sat up all night asking himself if there really is a dog. There is. I've met hundreds.

One day, after a near eternity in the Garden of Eden, Adam calls out to God, "Lord, I have a problem."

"What's the problem, Adam?" God replies.

"Lord, I know you created me and have provided for me and surrounded me with this beautiful garden and all of these wonderful animals, but I am just not happy."

"Why is that, Adam?" comes the reply from the heavens.

"Lord, I know you created this place for me, with all this lovely food and all of the beautiful animals, but I am lonely."

"Well, Adam, in that case I have the perfect solution. I shall create a 'woman' for you."

"What's a 'woman', Lord?"

"This 'woman' will be the most intelligent, sensitive, caring and beautiful creature I have ever created. She will be so intelligent that she can figure out what you want, even before you want it. She will be so sensitive and caring that she will know your every mood and how to make you happy. Her beauty will rival that of the heavens and earth. She will unquestioningly care for your every need and desire. She will be the perfect companion for you," replies the heavenly voice.

"Sounds great!" Adam says with a grin on his face.

"She will be – but this is going to cost you."

"Oh, how much will this 'woman' cost me, Lord?" Adam replies.

"She'll cost you your right arm, your right leg, an eye, an ear and your left testicle."

Adam ponders this for some time, with a look of deep thought and concern on his face. Finally Adam says to God, "Eh, what can I get for a rib?"

22
MORE MISOGYNY

A man comes home from work, sits in his chair in front of the TV and tells his wife, "Get me a drink before it starts."

The wife gives him his beer.

About 15 minutes later, he says again, "Get me a drink before it starts."

She does.

A few minutes later, he asks for another drink.

The wife says, "Don't you think you're drinking too much? It hasn't been half an hour since you got here and you've already had two lagers. I'm getting fed up with this. You sit there every night drinking and we don't talk."

The husband looks up and mumbles, "That's it started."

A woman accompanied her husband to the doctor. After his check-up, the doctor called the wife into his surgery alone. He said, "Your husband is suffering

from a very severe stress disorder. If you don't do the following, your husband will surely die.

"Every morning, fix him a healthy breakfast. Be pleasant at all times. For lunch make him a nutritious meal. For dinner prepare an especially nice thing for him. Don't burden him with jobs about the house. Don't discuss your problems with him, it will only make his stress worse. No nagging. And most importantly, make love with your husband several times a week. If you can do this for the next ten months to a year, I think your husband will regain his health completely."

On the way home, the husband asked his wife, "What did the doctor say?"

She replied, "He said you're going to die."

The room was full of pregnant women and their partners and the pre-natal class was in full swing. The instructor was teaching the women how to breathe properly, along with informing the men how to give the necessary assurances at this stage. The teacher then announced, "Ladies, exercise is good for you. Walking is especially beneficial. And, gentlemen, it wouldn't hurt you to take the time to go walking with your partner."

The room went quiet. Finally, a man in the middle of the group raised his hand.

"Yes?" asked the teacher.

"Is it all right if she carries my golf clubs while we walk?"

A girl tried a practical joke on a stranger who sat at the bar. She engaged him in conversation about the weather and then suddenly shouted at the top of her voice, "GO TO BED WITH YOU? YOU MUST BE JOKING!" Everybody in the bar looked in shocked amazement and the embarrassed man sidled away to a table in the corner.

The girl felt sorry later for what she had done and she came over to the man and spent some time apologising to him. Suddenly the man shouted: "£10 FOR YOU? YOU MUST BE JOKING."

A man placed some flowers on the grave of his dearly departed mother and started back toward his car when his attention was diverted to another man kneeling at a grave. The man seemed to be praying with profound intensity and kept repeating, "Why did you have to die? Why did you have to die?"

The first man approached him and said, "Sir, I don't wish to interfere with your private grief, but this demonstration of pain is more than I've ever seen before. For whom do you mourn so deeply? A child? A parent?"

The mourner took a moment to collect himself, then replied, "My wife's first husband."

An 18th-century vagabond, exhausted and famished, came to a roadside inn with a sign reading, "George and the Dragon." He knocked. The innkeeper's wife stuck her head out a window.

"Could ye spare some victuals?" he asked.

The woman glanced at his shabby, dirty clothes.

"No!" she shouted.

"Could I have a pint of ale?"

"No!" she shouted.

"Could I at least sleep in your stable?"

"No!" she shouted again.

The vagabond said, "Might I please . . . ?"

"What now?" the woman screeched, not allowing him to finish.

"D'ye suppose," he asked, "that I might have a word with George?"

23
ARE COMPUTERS MALE OR FEMALE?

Reasons to believe computers are female:
1. No one but the Creator understands their internal logic.
2. The native language they use to communicate with other computers is incomprehensible to everyone else.
3. The message "Bad command or file name" is about as informative as, "If you don't know why I'm angry at you, then I'm certainly not going to tell you".
4. Even your smallest mistakes are stored in long-term memory for later retrieval.
5. As soon as you make a commitment to one, you find yourself spending half your money on accessories for it.

Reasons to believe computers are male:
1. They have a lot of data, but are still clueless.
2. They are supposed to help you solve problems,

but half the time they are the problem.

3. As soon as you commit to one you realize that, if you had waited a little longer, you could have obtained a better model.

4. In order to get their attention, you have to turn them on.

5. Big power surges knock them out for the rest of the night.

24
HAIRCUTS

I have witnessed both of these conversations many times over. I did not make up a single word of either.

Women's Version

Woman #1: Oh! You've had your hair done! That's so nice!

Woman #2: Do you think so? I wasn't sure when she gave me the mirror. I mean, you don't think it's too fluffy looking?

Woman #1: Oh, no, no, no! No, it's perfect. I'd love to get my hair cut like that but I think my face is too wide. I'm pretty much stuck with this stuff I think.

Woman #2: Are you serious? I think your face is adorable. And you could easily get one of those layer cuts – that would look so good, I think. I was actually going to do that except that I was afraid it would accent my long neck.

Woman #1: Oh – that's funny. I would love to have your neck. Anything to take attention away from this shoulder line.

Woman #2: Are you kidding? I know girls that would love to have your shoulders. Everything hangs so well on you. I mean, look at my arms – see how short they are? If I had your shoulders I could get clothes to fit me so much easier.

Men's Version

Man #1: Haircut?

Man #2: Aye.

25
SOME SAYINGS

Some things just need to be said, mainly, it has to be said, by women. When we are sitting there, saying nothing, sometimes we are sitting thinking but mostly we are just sitting.

Life is an endless struggle full of frustrations and challenges but eventually you find a hair stylist you like.

Perhaps you know why women over fifty don't have babies? They would put them down somewhere and forget where they left them.

One of the life's mysteries is how a two pound box of chocolates can make a woman gain five pounds.

The real art of conversation is not only to say the right thing in the right place but also to leave unsaid the wrong thing at the tempting moment.

Time may be a great healer but it's also a terrible beauty therapist.

Brain cells come and brain cells go but fat cells live forever.

Life not only begins at forty, it also begins to show.

Just when I was getting used to yesterday, along came today.

If at first you don't succeed, see if the loser gets anything.

I had to give up jogging for my health. My thighs kept rubbing together and setting my knickers on fire.

Amazing! You just hang something in your wardrobe for a while and it shrinks two sizes.

The only time a woman wishes she were a year older is when she is expecting a baby.

Inside some of us is a thin person struggling to get out but she can usually be sedated with a few pieces of chocolate cake.

26

WHAT, EXACTLY, ARE THOSE CURIOUS ANIMALS CALLED CATS?

Meow!

1. Cats do what they want, when they want.
2. They rarely listen to you.
3. They're totally unpredictable.
4. They whine when they are not happy.
5. When you want to play, they want to be left alone.
6. When you want to be alone, they want to play.
7. They expect you to cater to their every whim.
8. They're moody.
9. They leave their hair everywhere.
10. They drive you daft.

Conclusion: Cats are tiny wee women in cheap fur coats.

27

TWO PUNCHLINES
FOR THE PRICE OF ONE

At last, after years of torment and frustration, the world premiere of the equal opportunity joke, tara!

A group of men and one woman are sitting together at the football. During the game the guys notice that the girl knows just as much about the game as they do, and are really impressed.

After the game they ask her, "How is it that you know so much about football?"

She says, "Well, I used to be a man and I had a sex change."

The men are amazed but very curious about the process. "What was the most painful part of the operation? Was it when they cut off your penis?"

"That was very painful but that wasn't the most painful part."

"Was it when they cut off your balls?"

"That was very painful but wasn't the most painful part."

"What was the most painful part?"

Punchline A: "The part that hurt the most was when they cut my salary in half."

Punchline B: "The part that hurt the most was when they scooped out half my brains."

28

THE FIVE QUESTIONS MOST FEARED BY MEN ARE . . .

This chapter should possibly be titled, "The five questions most feared by *married* men", as there are many more questions that men fear, starting of course with: "Are you married?"

1. What are you thinking about?
2. Do you love me?
3. Do I look fat?
4. Do you think she is prettier than me?
5. What would you do if I died?

What makes these questions so difficult is that every one is guaranteed to explode into a major argument if the man answers incorrectly (i.e. tells the truth). Therefore, as a public service, each question is analysed below, along with possible responses.

Question 1: What are you thinking about?

The proper answer to this, of course, is: "I'm sorry if I've been pensive, dear. I was just reflecting on what a warm, wonderful, thoughtful, caring, intelligent woman you are and how lucky I am to have met you."

This response obviously bears no resemblance to the true answer, which most likely is one of the following:

   a. Football.

   b. Cricket.

   c. How fat you are.

   d. How much prettier she is than you.

   e. How I would spend the insurance money if you died.

   f. Perhaps the best response to this question was offered by Al Bundy, who once told Peg, "If I wanted you to know what I was thinking, I would be talking to you."

Question 2: Do you love me?

The proper response is: "YES!" or, if you feel a more detailed answer is in order, "Yes, dear."

Inappropriate responses include:

   a. Yeah, yeah, shed-loads.

   b. Would it make you feel better if I said yes?

   c. That depends on what you mean by love.

    d. Does it matter?

    e. Who, me?

Question 3: Do I look fat?

The correct answer is an emphatic: "Of course not!"
Among the incorrect answers are:

    a. Compared to what?

    b. I wouldn't call you fat, but you're not exactly thin.

    c. A little extra weight looks good on you.

    d. I've seen fatter.

    e. Could you repeat the question? I was just thinking about how I would spend the insurance money if you died.

Question 4: Do you think she's prettier than me?

Once again, the proper response is an emphatic: "Of course not!"

Incorrect responses include:

    a. Yes, but you have a better personality.

    b. Not prettier, but definitely thinner.

    c. Not as pretty as you when you were her age.

    d. Define pretty.

    e. Could you repeat the question? I was just thinking about how I would spend the insurance money if you died.

Question 5: What would you do if I died?

A definite no-win question. (The real answer, of course, is buy a red E-type Jag and a fuck-off sized boat with the insurance money.) No matter how you answer this, be prepared for at least an hour of follow-up questions, usually along the these lines:

WOMAN: Would you get married again?

MAN: Definitely not!

WOMAN: Why not, don't you like being married?

MAN: Of course I do.

WOMAN: Then why wouldn't you remarry?

MAN: OK, I'd get married again.

WOMAN: You would? (with a hurt look on her face)

MAN: (makes audible groan)

WOMAN: Would you sleep with her in our bed?

MAN: Where else would we sleep?

WOMAN: Would you put away my pictures and replace them with pictures of her?

MAN: That would seem like the proper thing to do.

WOMAN: And would you let her use my golf clubs?

MAN: She can't use them; she's left-handed.

29
MEN EXPLAINED

Men are a misunderstood lot, which all in all is probably for the best. Women are better off not knowing that we eat with our hands the minute they leave the room or that we use their nail clippers to trim our nose hair. Better for them, better for us. Still, it's annoying that women spend more time and money trying to understand the minds of cats than they do wondering about what makes men tick. Which is why they'll never understand . . .

1. Our consuming need to own the biggest and most expensive version of just about everything
Our compulsive desire to drive off-road vehicles in cities and use corkscrews that resemble off-shore drilling equipment is well documented. As marketing targets, men are suckers for terms like "professional" or "industrial strength", because inside every man is the germ of every profession he ever imagined himself one day excelling at. Most of these purchases are

harmless, little more than childish wish-fulfilment played out at a higher testosterone level. But occasionally we go too far. The man upstairs from me once boasted that he had a filter which filled his flat with, "operating-theatre-quality air". I kept him away from my surgical steel steak knives.

2. Why we are so bad at shopping
We've never been trained to do it the right way. Supermarkets are like giant booby traps for males – which is why, if you send a man out to buy eggs, sugar and bread, you should not be surprised if he returns home with a case of wine, a pair of jeans and a tree.

3. The reason we don't like to discuss The Relationship
Most of us will find any excuse to dodge those conversations that start with questions like "Are you really happy?" and "Where do you see us going?" A relationship is a delicate thing, like an antique clock, and we know what will happen if we start picking it apart. Often our reticence will result in a lengthy conversation about why we have trouble talking about The Relationship.

4. Why we think we can fix things
Almost all men believe they can repair virtually

anything with a little patience. In reality, we're only half right. Men are extremely good at taking things apart – whether it's a dishwasher or an antique clock, a man can break it down to its most basic components in no time. Unfortunately, this is where our expertise usually leaves off, and we're mostly satisfied with leaving bits and pieces spread all over the newspaper on the kitchen table.

5. Men and video games

Women cannot understand how grown men can waste huge chunks of their lives zapping things off a screen. When a man repeatedly rings his girlfriend to say he has to work late and routinely comes home at two in the morning all glassy-eyed, she will usually take this as evidence of an affair – when it's more likely that a pirated copy of *Streetfighter II* is making the rounds at the office.

6. That sometimes we really are ill

When men get ill, women are generally united in their belief that we are faking it. This is based on a tired old axiom stating that men will never fully understand the agony of childbirth so deserve no sympathy regarding matters of pain, fear or incapacitation. For the record, it should be noted that all men are in a constant state of feeling slightly under

the weather just from being men. It's only a misplaced sense of machismo that forces us from our beds every day to go into work and then down to the pub for a couple of slurps of the only thing that ever makes us feel any better.

7. *The way we watch television*
Men don't just watch the telly, they plug right in. Once we're on the right wavelength, we can watch almost anything, including commercials, with a slack-jawed intensity which probably drives you crazy. Unfortunately for women, men cannot achieve this higher state without a firm grasp on the remote.

8. *Our sense of humour*
When women say that what they most want from a man is a sense of humour, they tend to mean something different from what we mean. Women will never understand the comic genius of your mate who can make beer come out of his nose.

9. *Why we're so boring*
Male conversation generally relies heavily on petty obsession, technical jargon, numbing detail and presumed expertise. Topics that women only feel the need to mention in passing become test-match-length debates among men. True, some of us are

able to combine a scintillating wit with a flair for storytelling and a nose for gossip, but we tend to reserve these talents for conversations with women. Between ourselves, the drive to talk at length about tyre pressure or *Star Trek* episodes is too alluring. Even if your local darts team boasted Socrates, Einstein and Oscar Wilde as members, you'd still probably have to discuss the fastest way to get to the motorway.

10. *The male menopause*

Midlife crisis, the seven-year itch, whatever you like to call it – women don't understand the seriousness of this condition, instead seeing it only as an excuse for a man to resign from his job, buy a huge motorbike and start a relationship with a woman a third of his age. As if there has to be more to it than that.

30
DRIVE YOU MAD?

I know that jokes and stories about women's driving and gossiping are cliches, but most cliches get to be cliches because they are true, don't you think? Anyway, Liz Lochhead, renowned feminist of this parish, says, "Women gossip, men talk." And am I quoting out of context and deliberately ignoring the irony? *Mais oui, mes amis*. As you do.

Due to pressure from feminists, Guinness have been forced to publish afemale version of the *Guinness Book of Records*. Here are a few excerpts:

CAR PARKING. The smallest space successfully reversed into by a woman was one of 19.36 m (63 ft 2 ins), equivalent to three standard parking spaces, by Mrs Elizabeth Simpkins, driving an unmodified Vauxhall Nova 'Swing' on 12 October 1993. She started the manoeuvre at 11.15am in Ropergate, Pontefract, and successfully parked within three feet of the pavement 8 hours 14 minutes later. There was

slight damage to her own and two adjoining cars, as well as to a shop frontage and two lamp posts.

FILM CONFUSION. The greatest length of time a woman has watched a film with her husband without asking a stupid plot-related question was achieved on 28 October 1990, when Mrs Teenie McTottie sat down with her husband to watch *The Ipcress File*. She watched in silence for a breath-taking 2 minutes 40 seconds before asking, "Is he a goodie or a baddie, him in the glasses?" This broke her own record set in 1962 when she sat through 2 minutes 38 seconds of *633 Squadron* before asking, "This a war film, is it?"

INCORRECT DRIVING. The longest journey completed with the handbrake on was one of 504 km (313 miles) from Stranraer to Holyhead by Dr Julie Thorn at the wheel of a Saab 900 on 2 April 1987. Dr Thorn smelled burning two miles into her journey at Aird but pressed on to Holyhead with smoke billowing from the rear wheels. This journey also holds the records for the longest completed journey with the choke fully out and the right indicator flashing.

JUMBLE SALE MASSACRE. The greatest number of old ladies to perish whilst fighting at a jumble sale is

98, at a Methodist Church Hall in Castleford, West Yorkshire on 12 February 1991. When the doors opened at 10.00am, the initial scramble to get in cost 16 lives, a further 25 being killed in a crush at the first table. A seven-way skirmish then broke out over a pinafore dress costing 10p which escalated into a full scale melee resulting in another 18 lives being lost. A pitched battle over a headscarf then ensued and quickly spread throughout the hall, claiming 39 old women. The jumble sale raised £5.28 for local Boy Scouts.

GOSSIPPING. On 18 February 1992, Joyce Blatherwick, a close friend of Agnes Banbury popped round for a cup of tea and a chat, during the course of which she told Mrs Banbury, in the strictest confidence, that she was having an affair with the butcher. After Mrs Blatherwick left at 2.10pm, Mrs Banbury immediately began to tell everyone, swearing them all to secrecy. By 2.30pm, she had told 128 people of the news. By 2.50pm, it had risen to 372 and by 4.00pm that afternoon, 2774 knew of the affair, including the local Amateur Dramatic Society, several knitting circles, a coachload of American tourists which she flagged down and the butcher's wife. When a tired Mrs Banbury went to bed at 11.55pm that night, Mrs Blatherwick's affair was common knowledge to a

staggering 75,338 people, enough to fill the Millenium Stadium.

GROUP TOILET VISIT. The record for the largest group of women to visit a toilet simultaneously is held by 147 workers at the Department of Social Security, Edinburgh. At their annual Christmas celebration at a night club in Newcastle-upon-Tyne on 12 December 1994, Mrs Senga Crabtree got up to the toilet and was immediately followed by 146 other members of the party. Moving en masse, the group entered the toilet at 9.52pm and, after waiting for everyone to finish, emerged 2 hours 37 minutes later.

SINGLE BREATH SENTENCE. A Glasgow woman became the first ever to break the thirty minute barrier for talking without drawing breath. Mrs Annie McGregor, 48, of Possilpark, smashed the previous record of 23 minutes when she excitedly reported an argument she'd had in the butcher's to her neighbour. She ranted on for a staggering 32 minutes and 12 seconds without pausing for air, before going blue and collapsing in a heap on the ground. She was taken to the Royal Infirmary in a wheelbarrow but was released later after a check-up. At the peak of her mammoth motormouth marathon, she achieved an unbelievable 680 words per minute, repeating the

main points of the story an amazing 114 times whilst her neighbour, Mrs Dolly Mair, nodded and tutted. The last third of the sentence was delivered in a barely audible croak, the last two minutes being mouthed only, accompanied by vigorous gesticulations and indignant spasms. Mrs Mair may well also be up for the nodding and tutting record, but it is believed that Ms Muriel Gray's accomplishments in this field may just pip her. Incidentally, wasn't Muriel great as the banjo player in *Deliverance*?

31
THE MALE RULES

OK guys, now you don't need to read that stupid 'The Rules' book or talk about it or them. Just leave a copy of this chapter taped to the telly. Oh, aye, and leave home, at least for a while.

We always hear "the rules" from the female side. Now here are the rules from the male side. These are our rules. Please note . . . they are all numbered '1' on purpose.

1. Learn to work the toilet seat. You're a big girl. If it's up, put it down. We need it up, you need it down. You don't hear us complaining about you leaving it down.

1. Birthdays, valentines, and anniversaries are not quests to see if we can find the perfect present yet again.

1. Sometimes we are not thinking about you. Live with it.

1. Saturday and Sunday = sport. It's like the full moon or the changing of the tides. Let it be.

1. Don't cut your hair. Ever. Long hair is always more attractive than short hair. One of the big reasons men fear getting married is that married women always cut their hair and, by then, you're stuck with them.

1. Shopping is not a sport. And no, we are never going to think of it that way.

1. Crying is blackmail.

1. Ask for what you want. Let us be clear on this one – subtle hints do not work. Strong hints do not work. Obvious hints do not work. Just say it.

1. We don't remember dates. Mark birthdays and anniversaries on the calendar. Remind us frequently beforehand.

1. Most men own three pairs of shoes – tops. What makes you think we'd be any good at choosing which pair, out of thirty, would look good with your dress?

1. Yes and No are perfectly acceptable answers to almost every question.

1. Come to us with a problem only if you want help solving it. That's what we do. Sympathy is what your girlfriends are for.

1. A headache that last for 17 months is a problem. See a doctor.

1. Anything we said 6 months ago is inadmissible in an argument. In fact, all comments become null and void after 7 days.

1. If you think you're fat, you probably are. Don't ask us. We refuse to answer.

1. If something we said can be interpreted two ways and one of the ways makes you sad or angry, we meant the other one.

1. You can either ask us to do something or tell us how you want it done. Not both. If you already know best how to do it, just do it yourself.

1. Whenever possible, please say whatever you have to say during the adverts.

1. The relationship is never going to be like it was the first two months we were going out. Get over it. And stop moaning to your girl-friends.

1. ALL men see in only 16 colours, like Windows default settings. Peach, for example, is a fruit, not a colour. Pink is a flower and a snooker ball. We have no idea what mauve is but we don't like it.

1. If it itches, it will be scratched. We do that.

1. We are not mind-readers and we never will be. Our lack of mind-reading ability is not proof of how little we care about you.

1. If we ask what is wrong and you say, "Nothing", we will act like nothing's wrong. We know you are lying, but it is just not worth the hassle.

1. If you ask a question you don't want an answer to, expect an answer you don't want to hear.

1. When we have to go somewhere, absolutely anything you wear is fine. Really.

1. Don't ask us what we're thinking about unless you are prepared to discuss such topics as Motherwell's chances for the Cup, the 4-2-4 formation or four wheel drives.

1. You have enough clothes.

1. You have too many shoes.

1. It is neither in your best interest nor ours to take the quiz together. No, it doesn't matter which quiz.

1. Thank you for reading this. Yes, I know, I have to sleep on the couch tonight but did you know that we really don't mind that? It's like camping.

And I get to have a wank in peace.